THE POETRY OF AUSTIN CLARKE

The Poetry of Austin Clarke

Gregory A. Schirmer

UNIVERSITY OF NOTRE DAME PRESS
Notre Dame, Indiana 46556

THE DOLMEN PRESS
Mountrath, Ireland

Published in Ireland by
The Dolmen Press Limited
Mountrath, Portlaoise

Library of Congress Cataloging in Publication Data

Schirmer, Gregory A.
   The poetry of Austin Clarke.
   1. Clarke, Austin, 1896–1974—Criticism and
interpretation. I. Title.
PR6005.L37Z87   1983   821'.912   82-40376
ISBN 0-268-01549-X   University of Notre Dame Press
ISBN 0-85105-408-0 The Dolmen Press Limited

Contents

Acknowledgments

A list of persons to whom I am indebted for help with this book must begin with Donald Davie. To him I owe my initial acquaintance with Austin Clarke's work and, more important, my gratitude for an unfailing generosity and kindness that carried me through all the stages of this project. To George Dekker and Kenneth Fields at Stanford University and to my wife, Jane Mullen, I am indebted for numerous editorial suggestions and improvements. In Ireland, Augustine Martin and Maurice Harmon of University College, Dublin, contributed significantly, in person and in their writing, to my understanding of Clarke. And I am especially grateful to Nora Clarke for her invaluable willingness to discuss her husband's work.

I also would like to express my gratitude to the Whiting Foundation and the Vanderbilt University Research Council for their financial support of this project, and to James Langford of the University of Notre Dame Press and Robert Burns, Dean of the College of Arts and Letters at Notre Dame, for their encouragement and support. Finally, I am grateful to The Dolmen Press in Ireland for permission to quote from Clarke's *Collected Poems*, ed. Liam Miller (Dublin: The Dolmen Press, 1974), and to *Eire-Ireland: A Journal of Irish Studies*, in which a version of the second chapter of this book first appeared.

FOR ELIZABETH AND MATTHEW

1
"The Literary Separatist": Introduction

On Easter Monday, April 24, 1916, Austin Clarke, a twenty-year-old literature student at University College, Dublin, was listening to his eldest sister play the piano in the sunny breakfast room of their house on Dublin's North Circular Road. They were interrupted by a neighbor with news of armed men marching through the streets of the city and rumors about an attack on the General Post Office in O'Connell Street. Clarke immediately mounted his bicycle and soon was pedaling past barricades that had been thrown up overnight throughout the city. At five o'clock, he was opposite the General Post Office, where he met Stephen MacKenna—self-made man of letters, ardent nationalist, and friend and mentor to Clarke. Years later, Clarke recalled that meeting:

> He had been there all day. He looked pale and ill: it was obvious that only the intensity of his own feelings and of the event itself had sustained him. The G.P.O. was already cold grey in the shadow and beyond passing heads I could see again, almost obscured by the great pillars, the watchful figures of armed men behind the sand-bagged windows. Clearly against the blue sky above the roof waved the flag of the Irish Republic declared that morning.
>
> Stephen MacKenna said little to me. Thought, emotion, could find no other end for themselves than the words "At Last". Certainly, neither of us mentioned any of those friends who, as we knew, must be at their posts, so near to us or somewhere else in the city. The historic hour existed with all its secret, countless memories of the past, in and of

1

itself, so that even the feeling of suspense and of coming disaster seemed to belong to a lesser experience of reality.[1]

The "historic hour" of the Easter Rising ended five days later. Driven out of the G.P.O. by fire and pinned down in Hanlon's Fish Shop nearby, members of the rebel Provisional Government that had been declared on Easter Monday conceded that they had no choice but to surrender. To most of their countrymen, the entire incident seemed madness—the desperate act of a small band of extremists. And even those nationalists who shared the convictions and hopes of the leaders of the Rising—men such as Austin Clarke—could not then have guessed that the romantically conceived and hopelessly executed insurrection that they applauded would one day be seen by many as the single most significant event in Ireland's centuries-old struggle to free herself from British rule.

For Clarke, an aspiring poet fascinated with the romance of ancient Irish legend, the Easter Rising pointed at least as much to the remote past of pre-Christian Ireland as to the uncertain future of modern Ireland's political relationship with England. "The age-old emotions stirred in our country by the Rebellion gave for a time another significance to our mythology," he recalled years later.[2] This rekindled interest in Ireland's rich past led directly to Clarke's first poem, *The Vengeance of Fionn*, published a year after the Rising. With its publication began one of the most remarkable literary careers in modern Irish writing—a career that spanned almost sixty years and produced, in addition to novels, plays, and literary criticism, a body of poetry that stands as a major contribution to twentieth-century literature.

The range of Clarke's poetry alone is impressive. It includes narrative epics such as *The Vengeance of Fionn*, religious lyrics, confessional and meditative poems, satiric poems and epigrams, erotic verse, and translations of Gaelic poems. It ranges, in subject matter, from the pre-Christian era of heroic Irish figures like Fionn to the medieval era of monastic saints and martyrs and, finally, to the contemporary era of decidedly unheroic Irish politicians and clergymen. But throughout his career, no matter what his subject matter, Clarke remained faithful to the impulse—so clearly expressed in his response to the Easter Rising—that made him look to Ireland's legends for his first poem. Clarke was, from beginning to end, an Irish poet, writing almost exclusively about Irish subjects, writing with the Irish language and literary tradition firmly in mind, and writing not for English, American, or French readers, but for an Irish audience. "Few have been more than he the literary separatist," his fellow-poet Robert Farren once said.[3] Clarke himself expressed this commitment in an essay written nearly twenty years after the publication of *The Vengeance of Fionn*, long after the heyday of the Irish literary revival that had generated worldwide interest in Irish literature. "Irish poetry has lost the ready ear and the comforts of recognition," he said. "But we must go on. We must be true to our own minds."[4]

Clarke was exceptionally qualified to talk about not having "the comforts of recognition." His unbending resolve to focus exclusively on his own country cost him much, in fame and fortune. Although *The Vengeance of Fionn* was received enthusiastically by English and Irish critics, Clarke's reputation quickly dwindled, and for the greater portion of his career, he worked and published in almost total obscurity; one of his most important books of poems, *Night and Morning* (1938), was published in a private edition of 200 copies, as were three volumes of satirical poems and epigrams later in his career. It was only in his last dozen years that his work attracted sustained critical attention outside Ireland.[5]

This critical neglect owes something to Clarke's position as a post-revival poet. By the time Clarke made his debut in the Irish literary world with *The Vengeance of Fionn*, the literary revival already had more than one foot in the grave. W. B. Yeats, continually rebuffed in his efforts to create a literature that would be national but not narrowly nationalistic, had essentially withdrawn from his Irish concerns into a more personal and subjective poetry;[6] George Moore, who had returned to Ireland in 1899 to participate in the revival, had retreated to England; George Russell (A. E.), whom Clarke once called "the spiritual centre of the entire literary movement,"[7] was caught up more than ever in social reform; the Abbey Theatre had begun its long and steady decline toward conventional peasant drama; and James Joyce, in *Dubliners* and *A Portrait of the Artist as a Young Man*, had pointed the way to a radically different, thoroughly unromantic notion of Irish literature in which Ireland, far from being the land that gave birth to heroes like Clarke's Fionn or Yeats's Cuchulain, had become "the old sow that eats her farrow."[8] All in all, it was a most inauspicious time for a poet who believed as fervently as

Clarke did in the validity of the native tradition for modern Irish writers.

And Clarke's fortunes did not improve with time. In the 1940s and 1950s, the distinction of being the most significant Irish poet writing after Yeats was granted most often not to Clarke but to Patrick Kavanagh, a poet who made his mark by insisting vehemently on the need for Irish writers to break out of the Yeatsian mold and its commitment to the Irish tradition, and by mocking those writers, including Clarke, who held fast to that commitment.[9] More recently, writers like Thomas Kinsella and Seamus Heaney, both more overtly cosmopolitan poets than Clarke, enjoy reputations in places where Clarke's name is all but unknown.

The critical neglect that Clarke's work has experienced is also due in part to the considerable shadow that Yeats cast over the landscape of modern Irish poetry. "Yeats was rather like an enormous oak-tree," Clarke said ten years after Yeats's death, "which, of course, kept us in the shade and of course we always hoped that in the end we would reach the sun, but the shadow of that great oak-tree is still there."[10] Of course, writers like Kavanagh, Kinsella, and Heaney as well as Clarke have had to contend with this problem, but it was especially troublesome for Clarke, partly because he began writing during the period of Yeats's greatest reputation and partly because Yeats, with his considerable influence, actively disliked Clarke. The cause of the disaffection between these two men is probably lost forever in the mists of Dublin literary gossip, but it seems to have had something to do with Clarke's friendship with A. E., with whom Yeats had broken, and, perhaps, something to do with Clarke's short-lived rise to fame with the publication of *The Vengeance of Fionn*.[11] Whatever the reason, not only did Yeats do nothing to advance Clarke's career, but he discouraged it; for example, he noticeably excluded Clarke from the important *Oxford Book of Modern Verse*, which he edited in 1936—an action that hurt Clarke personally and professionally.

But neither the problem of Yeats's shadow nor his damaging antagonism can fully account for the widespread critical neglect of Clarke's work. It is, rather, Clarke's belief that "we must be true to our own minds," his insistence on writing not only about the Irish but for the Irish, that has made his work difficult to export. Clarke's reputation outside Ireland today rests largely on a view of Clarke either as an exceptionally able, albeit quirky, local satirist, or as a poet with an exceptional capability for expressing in English verse the Gaelic dimension of the Irish sensibility. Both estimates lead to the same conclusion, and to the term that is inevitably associated with Clarke's writing: provincialism.

Yeats once said that a poet "can only reach out to the universe with a gloved hand—that glove is one's nation, the only thing one knows even a little of."[12] For Clarke, making sure that the glove fit was far more important than reaching out with it. The subjects that he chose to write about and the audience that he addressed are characteristic of the literary separatist committed to giving voice to the experience of his native country. At the center of almost all Clarke's work is the somewhat anomalous experience of growing up as an Irish Catholic in the early decades of this century and of trying to come to terms with the guilt and self-doubt that the Catholicism of Clarke's day inspired with such singular intensity. Moreover, the immediate focus of most of Clarke's poems is specifically, and at times exasperatingly, local. The satiric poems and epigrams of his later years, for example, often demand a detailed knowledge of events, figures, and places beyond the ken of most non-Irish readers. And, finally, Clarke's extraordinary ability to express distinctive qualities of Ireland's Gaelic heritage is quite likely to be lost on the reader unfamiliar with Gaelic literature and culture.

However, to dismiss Clarke as a writer of purely provincial interest is to do him a great disservice. Clarke's work deserves to be appreciated, because it succeeds, to an extent that the work of no other modern Irish writer succeeds, in expressing accurately the Catholic and Gaelic dimensions of the Irish sensibility and in describing the political, social, and religious realities of life in modern Ireland. But Clarke's poetry does much more than this, and it is in ignoring the universal dimensions of his work and his vision that the label of provincialism does him the greatest injustice.

A distinction drawn by Patrick Kavanagh is useful here:

> Parochialism and provincialism are opposite. The provincial has no mind of his own; he does not trust what his eyes see until he has heard what the metropolis—towards which his eyes are turned—has to say on any subject. . . . The parochial mentality on the other hand is never in any doubt about the social and artistic validity of the parish. . . . Parochialism is universal; it deals with the fundamentals.[13]

No other Irish poet of this century was more convinced of the "social and artistic validity of the parish" than was Clarke. Moreover, beneath the sometimes forbidding surface of Clarke's persistently Irish point of view is a poet motivated by a broad humanistic vision, a poet profoundly concerned with "the fundamentals" of human existence. The experience of being Catholic in modern Ireland is, assuredly, "of the parish"; but in coming to terms with this specific experience, and with the legacy of guilt bequeathed by a vision of man as essentially fallen, Clarke's poetry stands as an impressive affirmation of an uncompromisingly humanistic vision, a vision that celebrates man's inherent worth and insists on his right to moral, intellectual, and spiritual freedom.[14] The political, social, and religious realities of twentieth-century Ireland—the subject matter of most of Clarke's public poetry—are, again, matters decidedly of the parish; but Clarke's satirical attacks on Irish politicians and clergymen also express a broad concern for social justice and individual freedom and, in the face of the increasing homage that the twentieth century pays to a calculating materialism, a concern for the importance of distinctively human and nonmaterialistic values, especially human love. Finally, the most obvious manifestation of Clarke's belief in the "artistic validity of the parish" is his lifelong commitment to Ireland's Gaelic culture; yet Clarke's celebration of that culture calls attention not just to its uniqueness but also to the value that it placed on human dignity and freedom.

An indication of how Clarke's poetry expresses a faith in the validity of the Irish parish and, at the same time, deals with what Kavanagh calls "the fundamentals" can be found by looking briefly at the corpus of Clarke's poetic achievement. Clarke's poetry can be organized usefully into four categories, roughly corresponding to different stages in his career. In his earliest period, beginning with *The Vengeance of Fionn*, Clarke wrote narrative epics, based, with one exception, on the pre-Christian legends of ancient Ireland. *The Sword of the West* (1921) and *The Cattledrive in Connaught* (1925) represent an attempt, eventually abandoned, to recreate in its entirety the best-known of the ancient Irish sagas, *Tain Bo Cuailnge*. These early poems, though far from perfect, exhibit a remarkably sympathetic grasp of the Gaelic literary tradition from which they spring. Moreover, in emphasizing concrete detail and human character, these poems also express Clarke's view of pre-Christian Ireland as a culture in which humanistic values were respected.

After *The Cattledrive in Connaught*, the most impressive of the early narratives, Clarke turned to a later period in Irish history, the golden age in which Ireland became the center of monastic Christianity. Here Clarke discovered a way of expressing the tensions intrinsic to his own experience as an Irish Catholic, tensions that came to be central to his poetry as a whole. Clarke found in the world of medieval Irish monasticism an extended metaphoric vehicle that worked in at least two different ways: the spiritual integrity of the medieval church could be held up in striking contrast to the materialism of the twentieth-century Irish Catholic Church, and, more important, the severe asceticism of monastic life could be used to dramatize Clarke's concern with the tension between a strictly religious view of man as inherently corrupt and a broadly humanistic view of man as inherently good and entitled to freedom and dignity. This tension is documented most clearly in two books, *Pilgrimage* (1929) and *Night and Morning* (1938). The first volume is concerned chiefly with the conflict between sexuality and asceticism, between flesh and spirit. The second, frequently relying on a confessional mode, focuses mainly on the conflict between reason and faith.

As its full title indicates, the volume *Ancient Lights, Poems and Satires: First Series* (1955) marked another turning point in Clarke's career. The book appeared after a hiatus in verse-writing of nearly twenty years, during which Clarke channeled his energies into drama, writing verse plays and directing a local theatre. In the poems of *Ancient Lights*, and in those of the volumes that immediately followed (*Too Great a Vine* in 1957 and *The Horse-Eaters* in 1960), Clarke donned the Swiftian mantle of public poet. Most of these satirical poems and epigrams see the Irish Catholic Church as chiefly responsible for the curbing of individual freedom and the neglect of social welfare in modern Ireland. Although directed primarily at the institutional—and often alarmingly political—manifestations of the Catholic Church in Ireland, these poems essentially carry on, under a different and often less subtle banner, the struggle documented in *Pilgrimage* and *Night and Morning* against restrictions of man's freedom, be it social or individual, public or private.

Clarke continued publishing satirical poems in the 1960s, including relatively large collections of them in *Flight to Africa* (1963), *Old-Fashioned Pilgrimage* (1967), *The Echo at Coole* (1968), and *A Sermon on Swift* (1968). These later volumes also contain an astonishingly wide variety of non-satirical poems that, taken together with the narrative poems that Clarke published in the 1970s, constitute a fourth category of Clarke's work. In this group, most impressive are the personal poems, particularly *Mnemosyne Lay in Dust* (1966), a long poem based on Clarke's experience as a mental patient; the late narrative poems, published in *Orphide* (1970) and *Tiresias* (1971), representing a new effort to celebrate the erotic, an important element in all Clarke's work; and the free translations of Gaelic poems, in which Clarke's ability to capture the sound and spirit of Gaelic literature is at its best.

Despite this great diversity of subject matter, most of Clarke's poetry emanates from his experience as an Irish Catholic. "Irish Catholics have taken their morality from English Puritans," George Moore once said,[15] and the moral climate that Clarke grew up in on Dublin's north side early in this century was certainly marked by a puritanical belief in the evils of concupiscence and a fundamental distrust of human reason. Like Joyce a generation before him, Clarke wavered between an emotional attachment to the lavish rituals of the Church and a terror of its eternal and temporal powers.

In the first volume of his memoirs, *Twice Round the Black Church* (the title refers to the dark and towering Protestant church, still standing, two doors from Clarke's boyhood home at 15 Mountjoy Street), Clarke describes a striking incident that may have been the genesis of that terror:

> In Berkeley Road Chapel, I read the name of Father O'Callaghan over a confessional and kneeling down, waited till the last penitents had left. Then I opened the side door of the left of the confessional and found myself in the narrow dark recess and, in a minute, the panel was drawn back. I told my little tale of fibs, disobedience and loss of temper and then Father O'Callaghan bent towards the grille and asked me a strange question which puzzled me for I could not understand it. He repeated the question and as I was still puzzled he proceeded to explain in detail and I was disturbed by a sense of evil. I denied everything but he did not believe me and, as I glanced up at the grille, his great hook-nose and fierce eyes filled me with fear. Suddenly the panel closed and I

heard Father O'Callaghan coming out of the confessional box. He opened the side door and told me to follow him to the vestry. I did so, bewildered by what was happening. He sat down, told me to kneel and once more repeated over and over his strange question, asking me if I had ever made myself weak. The examination seemed to take hours though it must have been only a few minutes. At last, in fear and desperation, I admitted to the unknown sin. I left the church, feeling that I had told a lie in my first confession and returned home in tears but, with the instinct of childhood, said nothing about it to my mother.[16]

This encounter with the puritanical obsession with the temptations of the flesh, which occurred when he was seven years old, understandably left a lasting mark on Clarke.

At home, Clarke found no relief from the agonies that he was undergoing in the confessional and schoolroom. In his memoirs, Clarke says little about his father, a Dublin Corporation official who became superintendent of the Dublin Waste Water Company, but his mother had, he says, "that stern Victorian sense of duty which spread to our country in the second half of the last century." He adds, "So rare, so refined was this sense of morality which my sister and I drew from her example, that, in comparison with it, the religion of the churches we attended seemed gross."[17] This Victorian propriety eventually led to frequent quarrels over religion, to his mother's burning some of Clarke's books (including one by Francis Newman, the younger brother of John Henry), and to incidents such as this, recalled with amusement in *Twice Round the Black Church*:

Because of this moral delicacy, even our family prayers became an ordeal which grew worse with every year. We said the Rosary each evening and when my Mother gave out the first half of the *Hail Mary* to which we said the response, her voice always changed as she came to the last words, "And blessed is the fruit of thy Womb, Jesus." The pace quickened and she ran them together. When, in turn, we said them, we imitated her rapid sing-song. The sentence was completely incomprehensible to me, but I suspected that it was improper, although it had been first spoken by the Angel Gabriel.[18]

The parallel with Joyce is one that Clarke himself calls attention to in another passage in *Twice Round the Black Church*. He describes meeting Joyce in the 1920s and reflecting on the experiences that they shared (they both, for example, attended the Jesuit-run Belvedere College on the north side of Dublin):

> As he sat there gazing abstractedly through dim glaucous spectacles and sighing to himself, I was scarcely aware of him, for, in the intolerable circumstance of silence, a dismal force constrained my mind back to the past. The "Portrait of an Artist" had long since become confused with my own memories or had completed them and, set up by his recollecting presence, I heard, as in correspondence, the murmur of classes and chalk squealing on the blackboard until teeth cringed, saw the faces of boys that I hated and Jesuits in black soutanes, the brass candlesticks turned upon some common lathe that had seemed to him like "the battered mail of angels," and, with heart in shoes, I waited, having had, as I fancied, those thoughts that are forbidden by the Sixth Commandment, for the fatal sound of the sliding panel of the confession box.[19]

One need only think of the famous fire-and-brimstone sermon in *A Portrait of the Artist as a Young Man* to comprehend the terrible vigor of the Church's injunctions against human sexuality in Clarke's time. And one need only recall Stephen Dedalus's fear and shame at the prospect of confessing his sins of the flesh to judge the effect these prohibitions could have on a young mind. "Had it been any terrible sin but that one sin!" Stephen tells himself. "Had it been murder!"[20] The tension between Clarke's need to cast off this same oppressive burden of guilt, and the concurrent need to satisfy a deeply spiritual sensibility—engendered by the very religious upbringing that repelled him—is the major force behind Clarke's poetry.

Comparisons between Joyce and Clarke can, however, be pushed too far; the ways in which these two writers respond in their work to their shared experience—and to the country of their birth and the literary and cultural traditions that they inherited—differ substantially. However much the nets of Ireland may have kept their hold on him, Joyce was an exile, and his writing reflects his cosmopolitan inclination and awareness just as surely as Clarke's reflects his insistent commitment to things Irish. The reader coming to Joyce (or to Yeats, for that matter) can get by with a sketchy acquaintance with what it means to be Irish in the twentieth century. That is not true of Clarke. The distance between these two positions can, perhaps, be gauged somewhat in a comment that Clarke once made about mod-

ernism, a decidedly international movement in which both Yeats and
Joyce were central figures. "The problems of modernism," Clarke
said, "can have little practical value in this country, where our literary
development is so distinctively different."[21]

A search for the roots of the conviction behind that statement
might well lead back to Easter Monday, 1916, and the image of a
twenty-year-old aspiring poet standing outside the General Post Of-
fice in O'Connell Street. The spirit that made the Easter Rising
possible, and the spirit that grew out of it—the "terrible beauty" that
blossomed from the ruins of a defeated insurrection—can be found on
almost every page of Clarke's writing. Its most immediate manifesta-
tion surfaced the year following that day in front of the post office,
when, "working every morning in a state of recurrent imaginative
excitement,"[22] Clarke wrote his first major poem, *The Vengeance of
Fionn*, in a six-week burst of activity. He showed the poem to
Stephen MacKenna; MacKenna suggested he take it to Ernest Boyd;
Boyd recommended him to A. E.; A. E. liked the poem enough to
send it to the Dublin publishing firm of Maunsel and Co. Ltd. A few
weeks later, Clarke signed his first contract. His career had begun.

2
"A Mad Discordancy": Early Narrative Poems

The Vengeance of Fionn, published in the spring of 1917, was a stunning success, winning immediate critical acclaim from both sides of the Irish Sea. Previously known only as a promising student of literature with a handful of published lyrics to his credit, Clarke suddenly was being discussed in the same breath as the great Yeats.[1] "Not since Mr. Yeats first put on his singing robes has any Irish poet appeared with such decisive claim to be in the bardic succession," the *Irish Times* said.[2] Lavish praise, indeed, as was Stephen MacKenna's review in the influential journal *Studies*:

> Of this I will only say that in my judgment we have here the splendid dawn of a great poet. I do not hint at the author's youth; his work appears to me quite masterly, line by line and in total effect. Take the word in the kindliest sense—there is no youth in this work. It is mature splendour: this poet will live: he has dramatic quality, very intense; he has passion; he has an almost incomparable wealth of rich words; he has a strange power over the line, the cadence, the pause, the weight of syllable: and he has finally a certain quality for which "magic" seems too slight an expression; it is rather power walking in radiant beauty.[3]

And *The Times Literary Supplement*, six months after dismissing T.S. Eliot's *The Love Song of J. Alfred Prufrock and Other Poems* with a brief and hostile review, and six weeks after according the same treatment to D.H. Lawrence's *Look! We Have Come Through!*, devoted two full columns to an appraisal of *The Vengeance of Fionn*, concluding that Clarke's poem "is as original in conception as it is refined in execution."[4]

The one significant attack came from the Northern Irish poet Joseph Campbell, who flatly called *The Vengeance of Fionn* "a bad book."[5] But even this was turned to Clarke's advantage. MacKenna immediately rushed to his defense, labelling Campbell's review "the deliberate slaughter of a beautiful thing," and questioning Campbell's qualifications to pass judgment on the young Clarke.[6] The dispute raged on in print for several weeks, putting Clarke squarely in the limelight of literary Dublin.[7] "This poetic castigation was a useful lesson," Clarke later wrote of the incident, "and I could not complain because the controversy . . . sent the book into a second impression."[8]

Time has, however, tended to vindicate Campbell. Later readers have found *The Vengeance of Fionn* and the other long narrative poems that Clarke wrote in the first years of his career (*The Fires of Baal*, 1921; *The Sword of the West*, 1921; and *The Cattledrive in Connaught*, 1925) verbose, awkward, and, above all, marred by a near-fatal overdose of descriptive detail.[9] There is a great deal of truth in these charges; nevertheless, Clarke's narrative poems should not, as some critics have suggested, be dismissed entirely.[10] They contain seeds of his later work, they help define his vision of Ireland's Gaelic tradition (a radically different vision from that established by Yeats and other writers of the literary revival), and, finally, they exhibit, if not "power walking in radiant beauty," at least, in places, the marks of an extremely talented young poet.

Clarke was certainly not the first modern Irish writer to retell the legend behind *The Vengeance of Fionn*—the story of how Grainne, betrothed to the great chieftain Fionn, cast a spell on the young and handsome Diarmuid, causing him to run away with her the night before she was to wed. Samuel Ferguson and Katherine Tynan, two writers who figured in the early days of the literary revival, published works based on the tale late in the nineteenth century; Yeats and George Moore collaborated on a play about the two lovers that was first performed in Dublin in 1901; and Lady Gregory translated the original Gaelic tale, which is part of the Fenian Cycle of ancient Irish literature, and wrote a play based on it.[11]

One thing that distinguishes *The Vengeance of Fionn* from all these versions is Clarke's use of concrete detail to transform the godlike heroes of ancient legend into decidedly human characters. A passage describing Grainne's sleepless night just before Diarmuid sets off on his fatal hunting expedition demonstrates this:

> In the deep of night
> When all were slumbering Grainne woke from dreams
> In sweating heat and tossed the heavy clothes
> Aside and sat up in the silent gleams
> Of moonlight hearing watchdogs at the gate
> Begin to whine. 'The moon is strangely bright'
> She thought drowsing, 'it must be at the full,
> And the rain and wind gone from the sky . . .
> O I am hot . . . there is the splindled wool . . .
> And the three firkins.' She listened. Her bedmate
> Muttered from his sleep and started up
> Calling with a loud voice 'The hounds! They race
> And bell down Beann Gulbain. Look! the boar
> Bursts from the blood-wet bushes. Quick, my spear
> With the long silken sling!' She felt his breath
> Burning on her. 'Hush! Diarmuid, you only hear
> The mastiffs baying the moon. It is some dream
> The Druid-dark puts on you. I saw his eyes
> To-night.' But he muttered. 'I hear a fir
> Talking, talking. There is a little thing
> Gnawing at the roots. It will not stir.
> What is it that is gnawing at the roots
> And talking, talking there?' Then Grainne turned
> And pulled him on her hot breasts until he slept.
>
> (CP 5–6)[12]

No previous teller of the tale causes Grainne to wake "in sweating heat," with such arrantly earthy mutterings as "O I am hot," while her attention wanders sleepily from the weather to her discomfort to objects lying about the room. This fitfulness reflects her distracted mood, which in turn contributes to a carefully controlled sense of foreboding that builds throughout the poem toward Diarmuid's death. Neither would one find in earlier treatments of the legend such a detail as "she felt his breath/Burning on her," nor the highly specific and erotic description that brings this section to a close.

It is precisely this kind of specificity and eroticism that makes Clarke's early narratives significant in terms of his work as a whole. Such a detail as "then Grainne turned / And pulled him on her hot· breasts until he slept" looks ahead to Clarke's lifelong concern with the erotic and with fixing things in concrete terms. It also expresses Clarke's vision of pre-Christian Ireland as a culture in which sexuality—and, by extension, secular pleasure in general—is accepted without inhibition. It is this unencumbered acceptance of the implications of man's inherently sensual nature that Clarke sees as threatened by religious stricture, be it medieval asceticism or the puritanism of contemporary Irish Catholicism.

In describing how he came to write *The Vengeance of Fionn*, Clarke refers not to the work of Yeats, Moore or Lady Gregory but to a narrative poem written by the little-known Irish poet Herbert Trench, whose first poem, *Deirdre Wed* (1901), influenced Clarke greatly. Recalling his discovery of this work, Clarke said, "Instead of the muted music of the Celtic Twilight, I held in my fist a mad discordancy, like fifes, drums, brasses."[13] That "mad discordancy" (a phrase taken from *Deirdre Wed*) was precisely what attracted Clarke to Trench; in Clarke's view, Trench's realistic and objective treatment of the story of Deirdre's love for Naoise and of their flight into the wilderness (paralleling the story of Diarmuid and Grainne in *The Vengeance of Fionn*) was far more faithful to the spirit of the Gaelic literary tradition than was the "muted music" that writers of the literary revival, including Yeats, had composed from similar materials.[14] "It is possible," Clarke wrote in an essay arguing for Trench's work, "that *Deirdre Wed*, for the sake of its passionate energy and movement, pointed a way toward a truer representation of Gaelic myth. . . . The Celtic Twilight is beautiful in itself, but it can appear Gaelic only to those—and they are many—who accept with Napoleon the Ossian of Macpherson. The objective manner of Trench is as a fact more racial than the shimmering mists of Fiona Macleod."[15]

The objective manner of Trench was also more relevant to what was to become Clarke's life-long preoccupation with humanism. The world of Gaelic culture, entered through the hard objectivity of Trench as opposed to the misty subjectivity of the Celtic Twilight, was seen by Clarke as a world emphasizing essentially human values, focused not on some distant land of the imagination, be it secular or religious, but on *this* earth. The importance of this perception of the

Gaelic tradition for Clarke's early poetry, and the extent to which it differs from the view of Gaelic culture presented by Yeats and the Celtic Twilight movement, can be seen by comparing *The Vengeance of Fionn* to Yeat's first narrative poem, *The Wanderings of Oisin* (1889), also based on material from the Fenian Cycle. Yeats's poem celebrates the poet Oisin's attempt to move beyond human mortality into an imaginative land in which love is immortal; the poem has as its theme the power of the imaginatoin to transcend, however temporarily, an unhappy quotidian reality—a theme that runs through most of Yeats's early work. The theme of Clarke's poem is exactly the opposite: the destruction of human love by time, something very much a part of this world. Clarke's Diarmuid, facing death, asks Oisin to make a song remembering him as having escaped time's destructive powers:

> Tell that the clay of age could never creep
> Coldly around my heart nor did I sit
> Mumbling at a turf fire half blind with rheum
> And maybe groping feebly in the gloom
> Finger the leather breast of a dumb hag
> That once, O Gods, was the white Grainne. . . .
>
> (*CP*, 10)

And *The Vengeance of Fionn* closes with this description, spoken by a young girl, of the aged Grainne, seen after Diarmuid is dead:

> And I saw poor Grainne in the sunlight
> Wrinkled and ugly. I do not think she slept.
> My mother says that she was beautiful
> Proud, white, and a queen's daughter long ago,
> And that they were great lovers in the old days—
> Before she was married—and lived in hilly woods
> Until they wearied.
> I do not want to grow so old like her.
>
> (*CP*, 40)

The force of Clarke's poem depends largely on the degree to which Grainne and Diarmuid are portrayed as human and therefore subject to time's powers and to mortality. In *The Wanderings of Oisin*, on the other hand, Yeats's heroine Niamh is distinctly ethereal, and Yeats's description of her when she first appears to Oisin might be compared profitably with Clarke's description of Grainne waking "In sweating heat":

> When ambling down the vale we met
> A maiden, on a slender steed,
> Whose careful pastern pressed the sod
> As though he held an earthly mead
> Scarce worthy of a hoof gold-shod.
> For gold his hooves and silk his rein,
> And 'tween his ears, above his mane,
> A golden crescent lit the plain,
> And pearly white his well-groomed hair.
> His mistress was more mild and fair
> Than doves that moaned round Eman's hall
> Among the leaves of the laurel wall,
> And feared always the bow-strings twanging.
> Her eyes were soft as dew-drops hanging
> Upon the grass-blades' bending tips.[16]

The point is not that this passage is inferior to Clarke's description of Grainne (although it clearly is), but that it is deliberately less objective, less human, and, as Clarke would be the first to insist, less faithful to the Gaelic culture to which it claims affinity.[17]

This is not, however, to dismiss the weaknesses of *The Vengeance of Fionn*. The poem is often verbose and awkward, and the narrative line is frequently thwarted by adjective-laden description. One example will perhaps suffice:

> Through dark ravines of cloud the dawning broke
> In flashing cataracts of angered gold
> On eagle crags; in mists of greyish smoke
> The waters of the darkness, black and cold,
> Spilled from the world's cliffs to the ocean pit.
>
> (*CP*, 25)

Phrases such as "dark ravines," "flashing cataracts," "angered gold," and "greyish smoke" not only drag out the description at great cost to the narrative, but also, because of their abundance, blur rather than sharpen the visual image being sought.

These problems persist in Clarke's next two long poems, published four years after *The Vengeance of Fionn* had made his reputation. In fact, the charge commonly made against *The Vengeance of Fionn*, that its wealth of descriptive detail often interferes with the narrative, is far more true of these two poems—*The Fires of Baal*, based on Biblical material, and *The Sword of the West*, which turns from the southern Fenian Cycle of legends used in *The Vengeance of Fionn* to the better-known northern cycle built largely around the heroic figure of Cuchulain. For the 1936 edition of his collected poems, Clarke rearranged much of the material in *The Sword of the West*, and dropped some of it altogether.

Before he abandoned the legends of pre-Christian Ireland for the monasteries of medieval Ireland, Clarke wrote one last narrative poem, *The Cattledrive in Connaught* (1925), that easily stands as the best of his early work. This poem is closer to the "mad discordancy" of Trench's vision of Gaelic Ireland than anything that Clarke was to write for almost forty years. Moreover, its objectivity, energy, and explicitness, and its emphasis on human character, make it the most significant expression in Clarke's early work of the underlying faith in humanism that informs all his best writing.

The Cattledrive in Connaught originally was planned as part of a complete rendering into English of the most famous of Irish epics, *Tain Bo Cuailnge*, and it begins with the opening "pillow-talk" episode of the *Tain*, in which Queen Maeve and her husband Ailill quarrel about who has the most wealth. (The quarrel eventually leads to Maeve's unsuccessful efforts to borrow a famous bull from a ruler in the Cuailnge province of Ulster, and so to a major war between the forces of Connacht and Ulster.) Clarke's ability to inject these legendary figures with human qualities, his feel for concrete detail, his ear for dialogue, and his sense of humor can be seen in the opening lines of the poem:

> Queen Maeve sat up in bed and shook once more
> Her snoring husband:
> > 'And I cannot sleep
> An inch now for my head is full of words
> That spoiled the chessboard, held the drinking cups
> Half drained and climbed the more as candlelight
> Ran low and is there any doubt that I
> Had greater wealth when we were wed than you
> Had bargained with my hand—have I not filled

The west with lowing herds, have I not fleeced
The hills, have I not brought the middlemen
From grassing plains to lift a wondering head
From seaward clouds and count a rout of horses
Graze beyond swimming where few island women
Gallop them, bareback, to the little seas
Of Connaught? Have I now or have I not?
Tell me, have I not hung this draughty house
From family looms and put a golden bit
Upon the winter, silence on the floor
With rushes that forget their dancing, kept
The churn in clotty buttermilk, the cauldron
In bubbling oatmeal, spun the heavy flower
Of wool?'
          'Your sheep go through my gap
And there is sleep on me.'

                            (*CP*, 135)

The first line and a half, reducing the powerful king of Connacht to a "snoring husband" (a description that takes an added emphasis from the link, modeled on Gaelic patterns of assonance, between "more" and "*snor*ing"), sets the pattern for the poem's insistence on the humanity of these legendary figures. To a large extent, this quality is conveyed through dialogue. Maeve's long-windedness (her first sentence, for example, begins *in media res*, and runs on for fourteen lines, jumbling together a "mad discordancy" of events, figures, and objects), her insistent questioning ("Have I now or have I not?"), and her use of the imperative ("Tell me, have I not hung . . . ") all define her character—her need to dominate, and the insecurity that seems to lie behind it. Ailill's contrasting character, and his manner of dealing with Maeve's overbearing personality, are clearly indicated in his laconic line-and-a-half response.

This very human tension between husband and wife, little of which appears in the original *Tain* episode,[18] increases in the next exchange; Maeve is, characteristically, pouring into her husband's unwilling ear a description of her riches:

                            'You have not said
That I have greater wealth than you? Women
Can own their marriage-portion now-a-days

And is not mine the counterpane above
You, the door against the cold, has it not stored
The barn with oats and barley, ground white food
Out of the mill, cut down the heavy gleams
Within the woods and where the dawning smokes
From earthy skies driven the pale plough:
And rousing now, do you not hear my cows
Chewing in the new byre, the folded bleat
Of ewes that have been collied from the hills
In the red o' the year, while swine are in the oakwoods
And hookers riding by the hundred islands
Of Clew, heavy with running clouds or keeled
With wine—have I not brought into this kingdom
Larger wealth?'

                Flattening out the bolster
He said:
          'Aye, but you brought it all
Upon your back.'

                            (*CP*, 135–136)

The suggestiveness of Ailill's reply becomes more explicit when he next interrupts his wife:

    'Husband, men of the north have said
To-night that I am wealthier and . . . '
                        'Like
It is. A woman's ear is red for praise.
What of your wealth when you could never keep
The gate barred?'

                            (*CP*, 136–137)

The reference to Maeve's sexual proclivity is part of the sexual undercurrent that runs through much of Ailill's and Maeve's dialogue; and this undercurrent is not incidental to the poem, nor to Clarke's vision of pagan Ireland. According to that vision—and to the vision that informs Clarke's poetry in general—human sexuality is not to be repressed by censure, nor sublimated by the imagination (as it is in Yeats's *The Wandering of Oisin*); it is, rather, an intrinsic part of human nature, and is to be accepted, and celebrated, as such.

Although much of the descriptive power of *The Cattledrive in*

Connaught depends on the voice of Maeve, a great deal is supplied by the narrative voice. The confidence, energy, and vividness of this voice, evident in the following description of the gathering of goods in Maeve's house, mark a significant advance over the descriptive writing of Clarke's earlier narratives:

> The floor was piled with dross
> Of purple cloth, green hangings, golden shards
> Of wool. Bare shadows ran unfolding them
> Into a shimmering heap. There was a clatter
> Of scullions putting cauldrons in a row,
> Huge spits of iron tumbling from the chimney
> And wenches hurried in with raw red chilblains
> Upon their knuckles.
>
> (*CP*, 140)

The energy of image ("golden shards / Of wool," "huge spits of iron tumbling from the chimney"), of syntax ("bare shadows ran," "wenches hurried in"), and of sound (the alliterative links between "shards," "shadows," and "shimmering," and the more complex set of sounds in which "clatter" and "scullions" are echoed by "putting" and "cauldrons," reflecting the noises of the kitchen) all infuse this passage with a life that easily surpasses that of the clotted descriptions of Clarke's earlier poems. Moreover, the reliance on assonance rather than on rhyme, a technique characteristic of Gaelic verse, and the concern for objective detail, down to the knuckles of the kitchen help, place the passage firmly in the tradition of Gaelic literature.

Perhaps nowhere in Clarke's early work is the free-wheeling nature of that tradition—and of the pagan, Gaelic spirit that informs it—more clearly expressed than in this description of the fair that is held to celebrate the contest of wealth between Maeve and Ailill:

> . . . —but men
> Hammered the boards and laughing girls tucked up
> Red flannel petticoats around their forks
> And footed to the reeds, as washerwomen,
> The high-step jig; the boys tripped from the drink
> And caught them into sixteen-handed reels
> And grabbing hold of bolder wenches, big
> Of bone, with coarse red hair, shouting, clapping

> A gamey hand upon those buttocks loud
> And shapely as a mare's, they danced them off
> Their feet.
>
> (CP, 145)

The realistic and receptive attitude toward sexual pleasure suggested in Ailill's and Maeve's humor is unmistakable here. Also evident is a poetic control more characteristic of the mature Clarke than of the author of most of these early narrative poems. And, finally, one might also note how far these "bolder wenches, big/ Of bone" are from Yeats's Niamh, and how much more evocative they are of the spirit of Gaelic Ireland.

The image of those lively wenches being danced off their feet is central to Clarke's vision of pre-Christian Ireland; it also represents all the qualities that Clarke saw as threatened by suspicion, fear, and guilt with the advent of Christianity. It is precisely the tension between the generous spirit of those dancers at Maeve's fair and the intolerant spirit of religious prohibition set against it that is the focus of Clarke's next book of poems, *Pilgrimage*, in which he turns away from the "mad discordancy" of pagan Ireland to explore the more ordered, but also more pernicious, quiet of medieval, monastic Ireland.

3

"A Court of Judgment on the Soul" (I): *Pilgrimage*

In *Twice Round the Black Church*, Clarke quotes a passage from Ibsen that, he says, "gives us a definition of poetry which seems appropriate to our needs, more so than many of those well-known definitions which we borrow from English critics to our confusion."[1] The Ibsen lines are:

> Poetry—'tis a Court
> Of Judgment on the soul.

The poems in *Pilgramage and Other Poems* (1929) and in the volume that followed it nine years later, *Night and Morning*, certainly agree with Ibsen's definition; in these two books, Clarke tries to come to terms with his upbringing as an Irish Catholic, and in doing so, begins wrestling with questions that can be answered only in the soul.

Clarke's religious experience had pulled him in two radically different directions. On the one hand, the distrust of mind and body inherent to Irish Catholicism had generated deep-seated feelings of guilt and self-doubt, and, eventually, a desire to reject religious experience as anti-humanistic; on the other hand, this same religious upbringing had created an equally profound need for spiritual fulfillment. The poems of *Pilgrimage* and *Night and Morning* are the most effective expression of this dilemma in Clarke's work.[2] In documenting Clarke's efforts to reject the values and attitudes of contemporary Irish Catholicism, these poems assert with great conviction and force the humanistic appreciation of man's intrinsic worth and freedom that informs all of Clarke's work; at the same time, they recognize the

23

limitations of secular humanism, chiefly its refusal to look beyond this world for the purpose and meaning of human existence. Informed by this tension, these two volumes, although written out of Clarke's specific experiences as an Irish Catholic, address much broader issues that are concerned not with the provincial but, to return to Patrick Kavanagh's definition of parochialism, with the "fundamentals" of life.

As might be expected from a poet with Clarke's commitment to his native tradition, the court that sits in judgment of the conflicts explored in these two volumes is distinctively Irish, and Irish in Clarke's sense of the term: that is, Gaelic and Catholic. It is Gaelic partly by virtue of the assonantal patterns that give these poems much of their distinctive character. These two volumes mark Clarke's first significant experiments with assonance, and in a note written for *Pilgrimage*, he argues for the advantages of this practice:

> Assonance, more elaborate in Gaelic than in Spanish poetry, takes the clapper from the bell of rhyme. In simple patterns, the tonic word at the end of the line is supported by a vowel-rhyme in the middle of the next line. . . .
>
> The natural lack of double rhymes in English leads to an avoidance of words of more than one syllable at the end of the lyric line, except in blank alternation with rhyme. A movement constant in Continental languages is absent. But by cross-rhymes or vowel-rhyming, separately, one or more of the syllables of longer words, on or off the accent, the difficulty may be turned: lovely and neglected words are advanced to the tonic place and divide their echoes.
>
> (*CP*, 547)

A stanza from "Celibacy," a poem in *Pilgrimage*, illustrates some of these qualities:

> On pale knees in the dawn,
> Parting the straw that wrapped me,
> She sank until I saw
> The bright roots of her scalp.
> She pulled me down to sleep,
> But I fled as the Baptist
> To thistle and to reed.
>
> (*CP*, 155)

Here "dawn" and "saw" echo each other, "*wrapped* me" and "her *scalp*" create a cross-vowel-rhyme, as do "her *scalp*" and "*Bap*tist," and, finally, "sleep" and "reed" are connected through assonance. In addition, "dawn" finds an echo in "straw" in the middle of line two, "*wrapped* me" is linked to "sank" in the middle of three, and "Baptist" echoes both "her *scalp*" and, with its other syllable, "*thist*le" in the middle of line seven. This is by no means Clarke's practice at its most complex; he often uses true rhyme and cross-rhyme in conjunction with assonance, and complex patterns of assonance within a line.

The distinctive music that these patterns create is meant to reflect the sound of Gaelic poetry, much of which relies heavily on similar assonantal links. In these early books, Clarke was deliberately trying to depart from the English tradition, and express instead the Gaelic dimension of the Irish consciousness. "The verbal and poetic associations of the English language belong to a different culture," he once said;[3] in assonance, he argued, "we can find a legitimate means now of varying our medium to suit our particular needs."[4]

As Clarke found in assonance a way to recover the Gaelic dimension of the Irish consciousness, so he discovered in the medieval period of Irish history a way to express the Catholic quality of that consciousness. As a young man, Clarke cycled through remote districts of Ireland, inspired by some of the same pre-Christian legends that had excited Yeats in his youth. On one of those trips, Clarke had an experience that led him away from those legends and toward the medieval Ireland that spoke to an important part of his life:

> Having perfect faith in the Irish literary movement as I knew it, I had set out for the southwest of Ireland. I was on the track of the lost southern mythic cycle of Curoi MacDara and had a notion that in Kerry some imaginative experience might aid me. But something occurred to my inner eye. I could no longer see the rugged landscape of Ferguson and Herbert Trench, and another landscape, a medieval landscape, was everywhere I looked. I could not understand this intrusiveness until, suddenly, in Clare, turning the corner of a market place, I saw Scattery across an inlet of the Shannon. I scarcely saw either the island or its monastic tower owing to the silver blaze of water and sun. But I saw because of that light and in their own newness the jewelled reliquaries, the bell shrines, the chalices, and guessed at all the elaborate exactness of a lost art.[5]

Those jewelled reliquaries, bell shrines, and chalices reminded Clarke that the monastic church of medieval Ireland had produced great art and scholarship. As such, it could be contrasted to the Catholic Church of modern Ireland, which Clarke saw as materialistic and strictly opposed to learning and art.

But the medieval Irish church had another, far less attractive, side: the extreme asceticism of monastic life. In this aspect of Irish monasticism, Clarke found a way to express the conflict between human sexuality and spiritual discipline—a conflict that, for Clarke, was at least as alive in the Ireland of his own day as it was in the monasteries and hermit-caves of medieval Ireland. "The drama of racial conscience," he said in a note to one of the poems in *Pilgrimage*, "as strange to the previous Celtic school as Gaelic art, has become intensified. The immodesty of present-day female dress is denounced in virile Pastorals and Parliament passes laws against temptation."[6]

Medieval Ireland served Clarke as an extended metaphoric vehicle, then, in two ways—as a time when religion, in contrast to that of the present day, was devoted to learning and art, and as a time when religion, in a sorry parallel to modern Ireland, worked against natural human instincts. This period of history functioned especially well in the second way, partly because it contained the clash between the values of an extremely disciplined Christianity and those of the primitive, instinctual pagan culture that the medieval church sought to displace. The first poem in *Pilgrimage*, the title poem, depends on this tension:

> When the far south glittered
> Behind the grey beaded plains,
> And cloudier ships were bitted
> Along the pale waves,
> The showery breeze—that plies
> A mile from Ara—stood
> And took our boat on sand:
> There by dim wells the women tied
> A wish on thorn, while rainfall
> Was quiet as the turning of books
> In the holy schools at dawn.
>
> Grey holdings of rain
> Had grown less with the fields,

As we came to that blessed place
Where hail and honey meet.
O Clonmacnoise was crossed
With light: those cloistered scholars,
Whose knowledge of the gospel
Is cast as metal in pure voices,
Were all rejoicing daily,
And cunning hands with cold and jewels
Brought chalices to flame.

Loud above the grassland,
In Cashel of the towers,
We heard with the yellow candles
The chanting of the hours,
White clergy saying High Mass,
A fasting crowd at prayer,
A choir that sang before them;
And in stained glass the holy day
Was sainted as we passed
Beyond that chancel where the dragons
Are carved upon the arch.

Treasured with chasuble,
Sun-braided, rich cloak'd wine-cup,
We saw, there, iron handbells,
Great annals in the shrine
A high-king bore to battle:
Where, from the branch of Adam,
The noble forms of language—
Brighter than green or blue enamels
Burned in white bronze—embodied
The wings and fiery animals
Which veil the chair of God.

Beyond a rocky townland
And that last tower where ocean
Is dim as haze, a sound
Of wild confession rose:
Black congregations moved
Around the booths of prayer
To hear a saint reprove them;

And from his boat he raised a blessing
To souls that had come down
The holy mountain of the west
Or wailed still in the cloud.

Light in the tide of Shannon
May ride at anchor half
The day and, high in spar-top
Or leather sails of their craft,
Wine merchants will have sleep;
But on a barren isle,
Where Paradise is praised
At daycome, smaller than the sea-gulls,
We heard white Culdees pray
Until our hollow ship was kneeling
Over the longer waves.

                              (*CP*, 153–154)

   The poem describes a pilgrimage to several centers of monastic
Christianity in Ireland. But the pilgrims also discover remnants of the
pagan culture that medieval Christianity replaced. Thus, while the
poem pays tribute to the artistic and scholastic achievements of the
medieval church, it also suggests that those achievements came at the
price of an earlier culture. It also implies that some of the pagan values
supposedly driven out by Christianity have survived.
   In the opening stanza, the pilgrims first encounter a survivor
from Ireland's pagan culture: an ancient fertility ritual (the women
tying "a wish on thorn").[7] But in the striking comparison that closes
the stanza, the world of natural beauty that the visitors come from
(described in the first half of the stanza) gives way to the religious
culture of medieval Ireland. This mix of Christian and pagan occurs
elsewhere in the poem: in the third stanza's description of dragons
carved on the arches of Cormac's Chapel, the center of the Irish
medieval Church, and in the fourth stanza's description of the "great
annals" as embodying "the wings and fiery animals / Which veil the
chair of God." These annals, including the famous Psalter of Cashel, a
ninth-century manuscript that compared Irish with other languages,
often included historical chronologies and genealogies reaching back
to Ireland's pagan past.
   Despite these reminders of the pagan culture lying beneath

Ireland's medieval Christianity, "Pilgrimage" clearly celebrates the artistic and scholastic accomplishments of Irish monasticism. And it does so in a distinctive and appropriate way. In the second stanza, which recounts the visit of the pilgrims to an important center of medieval scholasticism, Clonmacnoise, Clarke uses assonantal patterns, modeled on Gaelic poetry, to imitate the art that flourished in such places. The dominant vowel sound of "a" in the first four lines— occurring in the internal echoes between "grey" and "rain," and appearing again in "came," "place," and "hail"—is replaced in the following lines by patterns centered on "o" and "oi": "crossed" and "*gos*pel," "*schol*ars" and "*know*ledge" (a terminal-to-medial echo that is a standard pattern in Gaelic verse) and, finally, "Clonmac*noise*," "*cloist*ered," "voices," and "re*joic*ing." The "a" sound does not, however, drop out of the poem; like the tail of a snake in a Celtic illumination that twists and turns in a complex pattern only to emerge at last, it reappears in "*daily*" in line nine and brings the stanza to a close in the final word "flame."

"Pilgrimage" also recognizes the darker side of monastic Christianity in Ireland. The world of stained glass, "sun-braided chasubles," and "rich-cloak'd wine-cups" is replaced, in the fifth stanza, by "sound / of wild confession," "black congregations" (versus the "white clergy" of the third stanza), a reproving saint (Patrick himself, no doubt, who is commonly pictured as driving out the sins of pagan Ireland), and the image of souls wailing with guilt and repentance on the top of Croagh Patrick. This shift is accompanied by a change to an assonantal pattern built around the bleak, closed-in sounds of "booths," "moved," and "reprove."

The poem ends with this aspect of Irish Christianity. At the close of the final stanza, the church that was celebrated earlier in the poem shrinks to the fading sounds of "white Culdees" praying "on a barren isle." Moreover, this vision is contrasted with the natural world ("light in the tide of Shannon") from which the pilgrims came, and with a world of material and sensual values (the wine merchants idling away the day in sleep). Nevertheless, although the pilgrims head out to the open sea and leave Ireland and its religion behind them, they do not leave it *all* behind them, as Clarke insists in the image that closes the poem. The religious allusion in "kneeling," combined with the suggestive adjective "hollow," remind the reader that religious experience cannot be rejected wholly.

Pilgrimage and Other Poems is largely organized around different perspectives on this unresolved conflict between Irish paganism and Irish Christianity. The poem that follows "Pilgrimage," entitled "Celibacy," takes the reader back to the white Culdees, but now they are seen not from the distance of a departing ship but from the inside of one hermit's consciousness, where the drama of racial conscience is raging:

> On a brown isle of Lough Corrib,
> When clouds were bare as branch
> And water had been thorned
> By colder days, I sank
> In torment of her side;
> But still that woman stayed,
> For eye obeys the mind.
>
> Bedraggled in the briar
> And grey fire of the nettle,
> Three nights, I fell, I groaned
> On the flagstone of help
> To pluck her from my body;
> For servant ribbed with hunger
> May climb his rungs to God.
>
> Eyelid stood back in sleep,
> I saw what seemed an Angel:
> Dews dripped from those bright feet.
> But, O, I knew the stranger
> By her deceit and, tired
> All night by tempting flesh,
> I wrestled her in hair-shirt.
>
> On pale knees in the dawn,
> Parting the straw that wrapped me,
> She sank until I saw
> The bright roots of her scalp.
> She pulled me down to sleep,
> But I fled as the Baptist
> To thistle and to reed.
>
> The dragons of the Gospel
> Are cast by bell and crook;

But fiery as the frost
Or bladed light, she drew
The reeds back, when I fought
The arrow-headed airs
That darken on the water.

(*CP*, 155–156)

This poem is more clear-cut than "Pilgrimage." The humor in the hermit's desperate efforts to escape the mental image of the woman is meant to be at the expense not just of a fictitious medieval Culdee but also, as the title of the poem indicates, of the modern Catholic clergy. Although firmly rooted in the medieval world, "Celibacy" looks ahead to Clarke's later anti-clerical satires, especially in such mockingly extravagant notions as "servant ribbed with hunger / May climb his rungs to God" (in which the ridicule is accentuated by the assonantal link between "*hunger*" and "*rungs*").

But "Celibacy" does more than mock the severe asceticism of the medieval Culdee and modern Irish clerics. It also suggests, by means of the pagan-Christian framework operative in most of the poems of *Pilgrimage*, that the demands of asceticism are unrealistic. The final stanza opens with the dogmatic assertion that the "dragons" of pagan belief and culture were cast out by Christianity ("bell and crook"); in reality, as the hermit realizes in the closing lines, those dragons are not so readily defeated.

Two relatively long poems in *Pilgrimage*, "The Confession of Queen Gormlai" and "The Young Woman of Beare," treat the flesh-spirit conflict from the point of view of a woman whom the monk in "Celibacy" surely would regard as an evil temptress. Like "Celibacy," both these poems attack strictly prohibitive views on love and sex, Queen Gormlai holding up the standard of love, and the young woman of Beare that of sex.

Gormlai, whose story is part of Irish legend,[8] married Cormac of Cashel, king of Munster in the ninth century. The marriage was not consummated, however, and when Cormac became an ecclesiastic, it was annulled. Gormlai then was forced into marrying King Carrol of Leinster, and the impotence of her first husband was succeeded by the lust of her second. Carrol eventually died in battle, but before that, Gormlai fell in love with her kinsman, Nial Glunduv, Prince of Ulster. After Carrol's death, Gormlai and Nial married, but Nial was killed not long after, leaving Gormlai alone and in despair. In his treatment of the story, Clarke mocks the unconsummated relationship with Cormac, disdains the lustful relationship with Carrol, and celebrates the love that Gormlai finally finds with Nial.[9]

The poem frames the story of Gormlai's three marriages with a description of her after Nial's death, lying alone in a hovel, "turning in straw and rags." The body of the poem is written in Gormlai's voice, addressed to a monk who has come to hear her confession. The monk hears instead the story of her three marriages, with Gormlai occasionally asking him questions that go straight to the heart of the church's views on love and sexuality.

Gormlai begins by remembering the years before her first marriage, years in which she lived as a princess amid royal splendor:

> With jewels and enamel
> Men hammer in black gold,
> In halls where feast was trampled
> And camps the battle-axe
> Had lit, I wore the crimson
> My women worked in pattern;
> And heart such flattering words,
> That I bit to the kernel.
>
> When companies came south,
> I was in too much pride,
> Counting the royal housework,
> Vats of red-purple dye.
> I had the light of linen,
> Blue windows in the sun
> To look from: I had thinness
> Of white bread and Greek honey.
>   (CP, 156–157)

This passage reflects Gormlai's state of mind, divided between her attraction to secular pleasure and her religiously inspired fear that these feelings are sinful. That fear is undermined, however, by the language in this passage. The argument that would condemn Gormlai is voiced in self-criticisms that have the dull ring of cliche and moral precept: "And heard such flattering words, / That I bit to the kernel," and "When companies came south, / I was in too much pride." These statements clearly are no match for the poetically rich descriptions of the luxuries and pleasures that Gormlai has enjoyed.

"The Confession of Queen Gormlai" also attacks the religious denial of secular pleasure through the character of Cormac, who bears an uncanny resemblance to the hermit of "Celibacy":

> His dogs had dashed a white stag,
> The day that Cormac bared
> Himself upon a flagstone
> And was alone in prayer.
>
> (*CP*, 157)

Unfortunately for Gormlai, Cormac carries these convictions to his bed-chamber, and the memory of this prompts Gormlai to ask a telling question of the monk:

> All night he turned to God
> Because the body dies;
> But had it been immodest
> For him to rest beside me?
>
> (*CP*, 157)

The poem does not, however, counsel an unlicensed attitude toward sexuality, as is evident in its treatment of Gormlai's second marriage. Carrol's lustful treatment of Gormlai is governed by an anti-humanistic urge to dominate and exploit, and Gormlai is seen as a victim of this drive:

> He drank at posted fires
> Where armies had been glutted
> And he shrank bars of iron
> Whenever his hand shut.
> At night was it not lust,
> Thought I were fast in prayers,
> For Carrol with his muscle
> To thrust me in black hair?
>
> (*CP*, 158)

The ugliness of Carrol's lust is conveyed here partly through Clarke's control of assonance. The force of the last line depends largely on the word "thrust," and the stanza carefully prepares the ground for it. Its short "u" sound is introduced in "glutted," a word with sexual overtones, and carried forward by "shut." The stanza's pattern of terminal assonance also calls attention to this sound by having "shut" and "lust" close two consecutive lines. Finally, the descriptive "muscle" picks up the echo again. These words all carry connotations of excessive force, and they come to bear on the last line, where for the first time in the stanza, the short "u" sound appears abruptly in the middle of the line, in "thrust."

The relationship that resolves the dialectic between Cormac and Carrol is founded on love. In recalling her feelings for Nial, Gormlai contrasts them to the unhappy events of her first two marriages:

> Two husbands had not fasted
> With me—and they were slain.
> One turned my soul at Cashel:
> His powerful foe had shamed
> The bed. All blame a widow
> That rids herself of grief.
> But, Nial, the day you rode back
> I came with oils and mead.
> (CP, 159)

The calculated suggestiveness of the final image here, like the earlier descriptions of Gormlai's life as a princess, overpowers the doctrinaire force of Cormac's asceticism and the degrading force of Carrol's lust.

The claim for the love between Gormlai and Nial is made most explicitly in Gormlai's final statement to the monk:

> Monk, if in matrimony
> The pair that has been blessed
> May please the lower limbs—
> My third bed was not less.
> I grieve our vessels shake
> The soul and though I grovel
> As Cormac in true shame,
> I am impure with love.
> (CP, 161)

The last line brings Gormlai's testimony to a close on a resounding note of faith in human love. Nonetheless, that conviction is not wholly free from doubt. For one thing, the tone of this stanza, up until the last line, is somewhat deferential. Also, Gormlai still voices the belief that "our vessels shake / The soul," that man, as a creature of this world, is fallen and, seen from the point of view of the soul, essentially evil. And she is still capable, like Cormac, of groveling "in true shame" for what she has done.

The poem also suggests that an outright rejection of religious self-denial may be not only impossible but also undesirable, a point central to Clarke's ambiguity about the conflict between his religious experience and his humanistic inclinations. "The Confession of Queen Gormlai" does not close with Gormlai's final assertion, but rather by returning to the perspective from which it began, in which Gormlai is seen alone and in despair after Nial's death:

> At sun, she lay forsaken
> And in red hair, she dragged
> Her arms, around the stake
> Of that wild bed, from rags
> That cut the gleam of chin
> And hip men had desired:
> Murmuring of the sins
> Whose hunger is the mind.
> (*CP*, 162)

Human love is, after all, transitory, and it has left Gormlai with nothing but memories and the fear that she may have been wrong, that her life may have been one of prideful sin. Perhaps for *that* reason she feels forsaken.

Whereas Gormlai would underscore the word "love" in her statement, "I am impure with love," Clarke's young woman of Beare would probably favor "impure." The heroine of "The Young Woman of Beare" stands as decidedly for the flesh as the hermit of "Celibacy" stands against it; indeed, these two characters represent the extreme poles of a dichotomy that is fundamental to Clarke's vision.[10]

"The Young Woman of Beare" is based on a tenth-century Irish poem entitled "The Old Woman of Beare," a dramatic monologue spoken by a legendary woman who had lived through seven periods of youth and borne fifty children.[11] Clarke's decision to call his poem "The *Young* Woman of Beare" is significant; whereas the heroine of the medieval poem speaks from old age and infirmity, lamenting the decay of the flesh, Clarke's heroine celebrates the flesh by recalling her erotic adventures with vigor and pride. As she says:

> It is my grief that time
> Cannot appease my hunger;

> I flourish where desire is
> And still, still I am young.
>
> (*CP*, 168)

Clarke's poem also deviates from the original in the contrast that Clarke draws between the heroine's eroticism and the religious life that goes on around her. This contrast is presented in the first two stanzas:

> Through lane or black archway,
> The praying people hurry,
> When shadows have been walled,
> At market hall and gate,
> By low fires after nightfall;
> The bright sodalities
> Are bannered in the churches;
> But I am only roused
> By horsemen of de Burgo
> That gallop to my house.
>
> Gold slots of the sunlight
> Close up my lids at evening.
> Half clad in silken piles
> I lie upon a hot cheek.
> Half in dream I lie there
> Until bad thoughts have bloomed
> In flushes of desire.
> Drowsy with indulgence,
> I please a secret eye
> That opens at the Judgment.
>
> (*CP*, 163–164)

The young woman deliberately courts the kind of temptation that the hermit of "Celibacy" tried to avoid. Moreover, Clarke's language works here, as it did in "The Confession of Queen Gormlai," against the asceticism that the hermit represents; the striking sensuality of the second stanza contrasts sharply—and favorably—with the literal and figurative darkness surrounding the people hurrying to church in the first stanza. This association of religious prohibition with darkness and of its opposite with light becomes a major motif in *Night and Morning*.

"The Young Woman of Beare" contains some of the most erotic poetry that Clarke, in a lifetime of such writing, ever achieved. Perhaps the best example is this recollection by the heroine of an affair with a "big-booted captain":

> Heavily on his elbow,
> He turns from a caress
> To see—as my arms open—
> The red spurs of my breast.
> I draw fair pleats around me
> And stay his eye at pleasure,
> Show but a white knee-cap
> Or an immodest smile—
> Until the sudden hand
> Has dared the silks that bind me.
>
> See! See, as from a lathe
> My polished body turning!
> He bares me at the waist
> And now blue clothes uncurl
> Upon white haunch. I let
> The last bright stitch fall down
> For him as I lean back,
> Straining with longer arms
> Above my head to snap
> The silver knots of sleep.
>
> (*CP*, 165)

The first stanza moves with a slowed-motion, almost hypnotic rhythm that reflects perfectly the smoothly controlled and pleasurable delays of sexual foreplay. The mood is shattered temporarily by "the sudden hand" at the end of the stanza, and the excitement of "See! See" follows. However, the image of the woman's "polished body turning," echoing the heavy turning of the captain in the first two lines, reestablishes the mood of controlled—one might even say professionally controlled—delay. The descriptions of the disrobing, in which clothes "uncurl," and the woman says, "I *let* / The last bright stitch fall down," continue this effect. Largely because of it, the climax of the passage, and of the lovemaking, comes with startling force, culminating in the sharp sound of "snap."

Like "The Confession of Queen Gormlai," "The Young Woman of Beare" is a dramatic monologue, and by modulating the tone of the heroine's voice, Clarke suggests erotic experience as effectively as he does through rhythm and imagery in the passage quoted above. In the stanza following that passage, the woman favorably compares her lovemaking with the experience of married couples:

> Together in the dark—
> Sin-fast—we can enjoy
> What is allowed in marriage.
>
> (*CP*, 166)

The confident tone of this statement begins to dissolve, however, in the next few lines, and approaches the questioning voice of Queen Gormlai:

> The jingle of that coin
> Is still the same, though stolen:
> But are they not unthrifty,
> Who spend it in a shame
> That brings ill and repentance,
> When they might pinch and save
> Themselves in lawful pleasure?
>
> (*CP*, 166)

At this point, Clarke marks a break in the poem, and when it resumes, the woman answers her question in a way that the clergy of her time or Clarke's would approve:

> Young girls, keep from the dance-hall
> And dark side of the road;
> My common ways began
> In idle thought and courting.
> I strayed the mountain fields
> And got a bad name down
> In Beare. Yes, I became
> So careless of my placket,
> That after I was blamed,
> I went out to the islands.
>
> (*CP*, 166)

The dance-hall reference seems a deliberate anachronism designed to remind the reader that the drama of racial conscience that the poem is describing has, as Clarke said in his note, "become intensified" in the twentieth century. In any event, the young woman appears to be making an effort here to see her life as it would be seen by the church.

In the next stanza, however, all this goes up in the smoke of her indefatigable memory, touched off by the line, "I went out to the islands":

> Pull the boats on the roller
> And rope them in the tide!
> For the fire has got a story
> That while the nets were drying,
> I stretched to plank and sun
> With strong men in their leather;
> In scandal on the wave,
> I fled with a single man
> And caught behind a sail
> The air that goes to Ireland.
>
> (*CP*, 166)

The false ring of the moralizing voice is gone, driven out by the vivid memories of an erotic life and by an irrepressible joy in sexuality. Just as the young woman tempts her lovers, those memories lure the reader away from the didacticism of the preceding stanza and toward the erotic experiences celebrated in this stanza, and in the rest of the poem as well.

After describing some of those experiences, the poem returns to an assertion of the heroine's pride in her sexuality, and the conflict between that pride and the church:

> I am the dark temptation
> Men know—and shining orders
> Of clergy have condemned me.
> I fear, alone, that lords
> Of diocese are coped
> With gold, their staven hands
> Upraised again to save
> All those I have corrupted:
> I fear, lost and too late,
> The prelates of the Church.
>
> (*CP*, 170)

Here again the young woman's tone resembles the uncertainty of Queen Gormlai; the power of her feelings, and of sexuality, is great, but so is that of the church opposing her and what she represents. As a result, the young woman fears not only that those whom she has "corrupted" will eventually be saved by the church, but, more important, that she herself, like Queen Gormlai, will ultimately be punished for her pleasures—that she is "lost and too late."

But the poem, unlike "The Confession of Queen Gormlai," ends on a note of defiance. The woman hears people returning from the religious services that they were hurrying to in the first stanza, and her mind turns to an image with strong sexual overtones:

> In darker lane or archway,
> I heard an hour ago
> The men and women murmur;
> They came back from Devotions.
> Half-wakened by the tide,
> Ships rise along the quay
> As though they were unloading.
> I turn a drowsy side—
> That dreams, the eye has known,
> May trouble souls to-night.
>
> (*CP*, 170)

The image of ships rising with the tide reflects Clarke's view that human sexuality cannot, despite all the efforts of "prelates of the Church," medieval or modern, be degraded or repressed. And the young woman's final wish is surely one that Clarke would second; indeed, the troubling of souls is precisely what "The Young Woman of Beare" is meant to do.

The gallery of portraits in *Pilgrimage and Other Poems* includes one other rebel, the hero of "The Scholar," a free translation of an anonymous Gaelic lyric.[12] The scholar's rebellion, however, is not sexual but intellectual, and so the poem looks ahead to *Night and Morning*'s concern with the conflict between reason and faith. "The Scholar" originally appeared in Clarke's first play, *The Son of Learning* (1927), based on a medieval Irish tale; in the play, the scholar exorcises a hunger-demon that has plagued the high-king, and his secular powers are contrasted with the unsuccessful efforts of an abbot and his monks, who, characteristically, have tried to starve the hunger-demon by forcing the king to stick to a strict fast. The poem celebrates the scholar's freedom—including his freedom from the church and its attitudes. Moreover, as a successful example of Clarke's early experiments with assonance, it does so in a style that honors the Gaelic tradition of which the scholar was historically an important part:

> Summer delights the scholar
> With knowledge and reason.
> Who is happy in hedgerow
> Or meadow as he is?
>
> Paying no dues to the parish,
> He argues in logic
> And has no care of cattle
> But a satchel and stick.
>
> The showery airs grow softer,
> He profits from his ploughland
> For the share of the schoolmen
> Is a pen in hand.
>
> When midday hides the reaping,
> He sleeps by a river
> Or comes to the stone plain
> Where the saints live.
>
> But in winter by the big fires,
> The ignorant hear his fiddle,
> And he battles on the chessboard,
> As the land lords bid him.
>
> (*CP*, 162)

After four poems that deal with the Catholic-Protestant, Gaelic-English conflict that was the chief concern of Gaelic bards writing in the seventeenth and eighteenth centuries,[13] *Pilgrimage* concludes by returning to the metaphoric vehicle of the pagan-Christian conflict of early medieval Ireland. The last poem in the book, "Wandering Men,"[14] also brings the volume to a close on a customary note of ambivalence. In the historical confusion between the famous Saint Brigid of medieval Ireland and an earlier Brigid, a pagan goddess of fire and poetic inspiration, Clarke finds the perfect vehicle for an equivocal response to the Christian-pagan, spirit-flesh conflict. Clarke calls attention to the confusion between these two figures in a note to "Wandering Men," and the entire poem depends on it:[15]

When sudden night had trapped the wood,
We stumbled by dark earthing
To find a path we never knew
Though we went down on bare knee.
But as we prayed there came a sound
Of canticles upon the air,
A momentary flame that rounded
The bell-house of Kildare.

Among her women on the threshold
Great Brigid gave us welcome.
She had concealed in colder veil
Too soon the flaming of her forehead
That drew our eyelids in the wood.
By shadowy arch she led the way,
She brought us to a lighted room
And served each one at table.

I think it was the food of Eden
We shared, for that new ale,
Though brighter than the serpent-reed,
Was not indeed of summer's brew,
And drowsily we heard the calling
Of voices from an instrument—
Soft as the music that King Saul
Had feared beyond his tent.

And all that night I was aware
Of shapes no priest can see,
The centaur at a house of prayer,
The sceptred strangers from the East.
Confined in dreams we saw again
How Brigid, while her women slept
Around her, templed by the flame,
Sat in a carven chair.

We wakened with the early blackbird
Before the oaks had drawn
An old sun-circle in the grass:

> The sightly house was gone.
> Yet we gave praise to that sky-woman
> For wayfare and a vision shown
> At night to harmless men who have
> No parish of their own.
> (*CP*, 177–178)

At first glance, the house that the lost men, who are obviously religious ("we went down on bare knee"), come upon seems that of Saint Brigid—the "bell-house of Kildare." The image of the earlier, pagan Brigid begins to surface, however, in the second stanza ("the flaming of her forehead"), and in the third stanza, with its sudden wealth of imagery and assonantal patterns, the pagan world of Brigid the fire goddess fully eclipses the religious world of Brigid the medieval saint.[16] The poem them combines both worlds in a striking image:

> And all that night I was aware
> Of shapes no priest can see,
> The centaur at a house of prayer.

"The centaur at a house of prayer"—perhaps in no other single line or image does Clarke so successfully express the impossibility of resolving the pagan-Christian dichotomy, or the broader flesh-spirit conflict that it represents.

At the end of "Pilgrimage," the first poem in this volume, the pilgrims leave behind them the Ireland of medieval Christianity, but they do not go empty-handed; their visits to religious shrines represent an attempt to respond to deep-seated spiritual needs, and, as the final image of the "kneeling ship" makes clear, the attempt succeeds to some extent. In "Wandering Men," the last poem of this volume, the "pilgrims" wake to find the house of the pagan goddess gone. But although they return to a world in which the first response of men lost in a wood is to pray for deliverance, their pagan experience has had its effect: "Yet we gave praise to that sky-woman / For wayfare and a vision shown." One needs, it seems, both centaur and house of prayer. Yet nowhere is it more painfully obvious that such a combination is not always possible than in the next volume of Clarke's poems, *Night and Morning.*

4
"A Court of Judgment on the Soul" (II): *Night and Morning*

"I have a feeling in reading this last book," Padraic Colum wrote in 1930 of *Pilgrimage*, "that the purely Gaelic spirit that delights in pattern for its own sake, and delights in what is esoteric, has reached a limit in these memorable poems."[1] Although Clarke could not have agreed wholly with this statement, especially its contention that *Pilgrimage* consisted mainly of esoteric exercises in "pattern for its own sake," he did seem to feel in the 1930s a need to break new ground. The result was *Night and Morning*, published nine years after *Pilgrimage* appeared. In this volume the medieval monastic backdrop of *Pilgrimage*, the frequent reliance on personae, and the concern with the opposition between sexuality and asceticism give way to poems that rely chiefly on the confessional mode and that explore the conflict between man's reason and religious doctrines that would repress it. But although these two books differ, they are related in a significant way. The tension between reason and religion that is at the center of *Night and Morning* is closely connected, in Clarke's vision, to the flesh-spirit conflict that informs *Pilgrimage*; both are seen by Clarke as aspects of an overarching conflict between a generally humanistic philosophy and a narrowly religious one, between a view of man as inherently capable of great achievement and entitled to the pleasures of secular life, and a view of man as helpless without the grace of God and in need of severe moral discipline.

Like *Pilgrimage*, *Night and Morning* grows out of Clarke's experience with the rigidly puritanical philosophy of the Irish Catholic Church, which, in Clarke's view, distrusted the mind as well as the body. "Having been trained by Jesuits from the age of seven," Clarke wrote in *Twice Round the Black Church*, "I am still unable to hold opinions with certainty and envy those who can trust in private judgment."[2] The other pole of this religion-reason dichotomy is described by Clarke at the end of *Twice Round the Black Church*, in which he recounts his emergence from the shadow of his faith, and concludes with this statement: "I watched frequently the Tree of Knowledge and—whether my eyes were closed or wide open—its bark and all its boughs were glittering."[3] That Tree of Knowledge, and the clash between it and Clarke's religious upbringing, stand behind almost all the poems in *Night and Morning*.

Perhaps the most complete statement of the central theme of the book is made in "Tenebrae," a poem that also reflects the stylistic changes that distinguish *Night and Morning* from Clarke's preceding work:

> This is the hour that we must mourn
> With tallows on the black triangle,
> Night has a napkin deep in fold
> To keep the cup; yet who dare pray
> If all in reason should be lost, ·
> The agony of man betrayed
> At every station of the cross?
>
> O when the forehead is too young,
> Those centuries of mortal anguish,
> Dabbed by a consecrated thumb
> That crumbles into dust, will bring
> Despair with all that we can know;
> And there is nothing left to sing,
> Remembering our innocence.
>
> I hammer on that common door,
> Too frantic in my superstition,
> Transfix with nails that I have broken,
> The angry notice of the mind.
> Close as the thought that suffers him,
> The habit every man in time
> Must wear beneath his ironed shirt.

An open mind disturbs the soul,
And in disdain I turn my back
Upon the sun that makes a show
Of half the world, yet still deny
The pain that lives within the past,
The flame sinking upon the spike,
Darkness that man must dread at last.

                              (*CP*, 183)

The change in style from *Pilgrimage* is immediately evident; the vivid descriptions, abundant images, and rich sound patterns built up by assonance give way to a much more austere voice—more direct, more compact, more crabbed even. The smooth, erotic rhythms of poems like "The Young Woman of Beare" are replaced by a more deliberate movement that encourages the slower reading demanded by the complex argument of the poem. And finally, the poem frankly relies on abstract terms such as "reason" and "thought." All these characteristics reflect the intellectual nature of the poem, and indeed the new style that marks *Night and Morning* as a whole underscores the book's concern with the struggle between religion and reason rather than the flesh-spirit conflict explored in *Pilgrimage*.

The opposition between religious faith and human reason is embodied in the division of the opening stanza of "Tenebrae." The first three-and-a-half lines, describing both the Catholic Holy Week ritual of Tenebrae and what it symbolizes, the Apostles' desertion of Christ during His passion ("Remove this cup from me: nevertheless, not my will but thine be done"[4]), are cloaked in the atmosphere of darkness associated with religion throughout the poem. (The title *Night and Morning* insists on the association of religion with darkness and reason with light.) Occurring precisely in the middle of the stanza, "yet" works as a pivot, turning the stanza away from the view that, because of man's guilt, "we must mourn" for Christ's suffering and toward the argument made in the second half of the stanza that such convictions are held at great cost to man's reason. "Tenebrae" was entitled "A Song in Lent" when first published in a London periodical,[5] and this part of the stanza works through a reversal of the doctrine behind another Lenten ritual, the stations of the cross. This ritual, in which worshipers visit various icons in the church depicting the story of Christ's passion, is meant to remind man that his betrayal of God through sin caused Christ's death on the cross. But in Clarke's version, it is man who stands to be betrayed by surrendering his reason to religion.

The poem's argument is, however, considerably more complex than this, and reflects the ambiguity toward religious experience expressed in *Pilgrimage*. For one thing, as the third stanza insists, religion cannot be dismissed so readily. Comparing himself to Martin Luther trying to post "the angry notice of the mind" on the door of a religion that would prohibit the free exercise of reason, the speaker concedes that such efforts must fail; the need for spiritual life is essential to man's nature, a "habit" (alluding to the habits worn by members of religious orders) that every man must wear beneath the shirt of his secular self.

The last stanza takes this argument a step further, suggesting that it is not only impossible to reject religious experience, but also, perhaps, undesirable. The stanza is constructed precisely as the first, dividing on the word "yet." But whereas the first stanza begins with religion and moves to reason, implying a rejection of the first for the second, the order is reversed in the last stanza, and no such rejection is proposed. In the first half of the stanza, the speaker disavows a total reliance on reason, conceding that it illuminates only "half the world." But in the second half of the stanza, he faces the paradox that sounds such a disturbing note throughout Clarke's religious poetry. While conceding the limitations of reason, the narrator cannot turn confidently to religion to satisfy the spiritual needs that fall outside reason's power; limited as it is, his reason inevitably produces religious doubt, and so he must "still deny" religious faith, that "pain that lives within the past." In the final line, the increasing darkness of the "napkin deep in fold" over the chalice, the darkness in the Garden of Gethsemane as the Apostles began to desert Christ, and the darkness of the cross of ashes in the Ash Wednesday ritual mentioned in the second stanza all come together with resonating force. This "darkness that man must dread at last" is no longer merely that of an anti-rational religious faith, but is now also the darkness of death and of spiritual despair. As the stanza moves to its close in a series of appositional statements, the force of the word "deny" shrinks with the growing distance from its object, and the poem ends not on the one-dimensional note of man's need to reject religious faith but rather on the more profound note, heightened by the rare rhyme between "last" and "past," of the possible consequences of such a rejection.

In "Repentance," a poem modeled on Gaelic confessional poetry, Clarke carries this point forward by insisting on the extent to which religious belief plays on the fear of such consequences:

> When I was younger than the soul
> That wakes me now at night, I saw
> The mortal mind in such a glory—
> All knowledge was in Connaught.
> I crossed the narrows of earthward light,
> The rain, noon-set along the mountain,
> And I forgot the scale of thought,
> Man's lamentation, Judgment hour
> That hides the sun in the waters.
>
> But as I stumbled to the flint
> Where blessed Patric drove a crowd
> Of fiends that roared like cattlemen,
> Until they stamped themselves out
> Between the fiery pens, I felt
> Repentance gushing from the rock;
> For I had made a bad confession
> Once, feared to name in ugly box
> The growing pains of flesh.
>
> I count the sorrowful mysteries
> Of earth before the celebrant
> Has turned to wash his mouth in wine.
> The soul is confined to a holy vessel,
> And intellect less than desire.
> O I will stay to the last Gospel,
> Cupping my heart with prayer:
> Knuckle and knee are all we know
> When the mind is half despairing.
>
> No story handed down in Connaught
> Can cheat a man, nor any learning
> Keep the fire in, turn his folly
> From thinking of that book in Heaven.
> Could I unbutton mad thought, quick-save

My skin, if I were caught at last
Without my soul and dragged to torment,
Ear-drumming in that dreadful place
Where the sun hides in the waters?

(*CP*, 186–187)

As evidenced by the nature of his first religious experience, the speaker's faith rests chiefly on an anti-rational fear of eternal punishment, the "Judgment hour / That hides the sun in the waters." This experience took the form of an epiphany at Croagh Patrick, the center of religious pilgrimage in the west of Ireland associated by Clarke in "Pilgrimage" with the fanatically ascetic side of medieval Christianity, and the terms used to describe the experience are telling: "I *felt* / Repentance *gushing* from the rock." That his faith is grounded in terror is also underscored by the reference to the legend of Saint Patrick wrestling with demons and evil spirits, and by the speaker's memories of not confessing the failure of his own struggles with the "growing pains of flesh." The inevitable shallowness of religious belief established on such feelings is advanced in the final stanza, in which the repentance that the speaker felt on Croagh Patrick degenerates into hypocritical speculations about deathbed repentance.

Although "Repentance" mocks the narrator's religious feelings, it does not undervalue the force of the fear that inspired them, as attested to by the somber note on which the poem ends. This note dominates *Night and Morning*. Words like "agony," "despair," "tormented," "dread," "pain," and "anguish" occur with almost monotonous frequency. And, as "Tenebrae" suggests, man inevitably suffers this kind of anguish because the conflict between faith and reason is fought across an unbridgeable gulf. The opening stanza of the first poem in the collection, "Night and Morning," explicitly defines that gulf and the pain that it causes:

. . . Thought can but share
Belief—and the tormented soul,
Changing confession to despair,
Must wear a borrowed robe.

(*CP*, 181)

"Thought can but share belief," because it is permanently separated from the spiritual arena. But thought also prevents belief, leading "the tormented soul" away from a full acceptance of faith to the despair of spiritual limbo.[6]

Two poems in *Night and Morning* look back to historical periods when that gulf was not so wide as it seemed to a twentieth-century Irish Catholic. In "Night and Morning," Clarke celebrates the Reformation as a period in which religion accepted reason:

> O when all Europe was astir
> With echo of learned controversy,
> The voice of logic led the choir.
> Such quality was in all being,
> The forks of heaven and this earth
> Had met, town-walled, in mortal view
> And in the pride that we ignore,
> The holy rage of argument,
> God was made man once more.
>
>   (*CP*, 182)

Unlike the Catholicism of Clarke's upbringing, religion in the Reformation is portrayed here as relying not on anti-rational faith but on man's intellectual powers, "the pride that we [in the present] ignore." And so the gap between religion and reason was, if not completely bridged, at least narrow enough to enable the forks of heaven and earth to meet, and to do so "in mortal view." The result, the poem suggests, was a kind of incarnation: "God was made man once more," made, that is, accessible to man.

In "The Lucky Coin," Clarke describes a period in Irish history, the days before Catholic Emancipation in 1829, in which the church was a much less effective enemy of humanistic values than was the church of Clarke's time. If the Counter Reformation hardened church attitudes against humanism in sixteenth-century Europe, in Ireland, Catholic Emancipation, by bringing an end to the Penal Laws of the eighteenth century, gave the Catholic Church new power and influence, which, in Clarke's view, were used to repress rather than emancipate. The "lucky coin" of the poem's title symbolizes freedom from the church's influence in the secular world:

> Collect the silver on a Sunday,
> Weigh the pennies of the poor,
> His soul can make a man afraid
> And yet thought will endure.

But who can find by any chance
A coin of different shape
That never came from Salamanca
Or danced on chapel plate?

Though time is slipping through all fingers
And body dare not stay,
That lucky coin, I heard men tell it,
Had glittered once in Galway
And crowds were elbowing the spirit
While every counter shone,
Forgetting grief until the ages
Had changed it for a song.

Turning in cartwheels on the fairground,
The sun was hastier—
That strolling girls might have for dowry,
Two hands about a waist;
Men voted for the Liberator
After the booths were closed
And only those in failing health
Remembered their own souls.

On Nephin many a knot was tied,
The sweet in tongue made free there,
Lovers forgot on the mountain-side
The stern law of the clergy
That kiss, pinch, squeeze, hug, smack denied,
Forgot the evil, harm
And scandal that comes closer, lying
In one another's arms.

Not one of us will ever find
That coin of different shape
For it was lost before our rising
Or stolen—as some say.
But when our dread of the unseen
Has rifled hole and corner,
How shall we praise the men that freed us
From everything but thought.

(CP, 187–188)

Clarke's characteristically energetic and explicit description of the secular pleasures enjoyed in the days when the Irish could find a coin that "never came from Salamanca" (a seminary in Spain that served as a center for training Irish priests during the Penal Days) recalls the description of the fair in *The Cattledrive in Connaught*. It is, however, countered by the sobering thought that, now, "not one of us will ever find / That coin of different shape"—that, paradoxically, the Irish are less free after Emancipation than they were before the achievements of Daniel O'Connell and other "men that freed us." Living under the thumb of an increasingly powerful church that disapproves of secular pleasures and distrusts reason, the modern Irishman, Clarke says, must face the dilemma that is the principal theme of *Night and Morning*: "His soul can make a man afraid / And yet thought will endure."

"Penal Law," which looks ahead to Clarke's later satirical attacks on the church, uses the same idea of the Irish as having traded one kind of tyranny for another in ridding themselves of the Penal Laws (and, eventually, of British domination in general) while accepting the growing authority of the Catholic Church:

> Burn Ovid with the rest. Lovers will find
> A hedge-school for themselves and learn by heart
> All that the clergy banish from the mind,
> When hands are joined and head bows in the dark.
>
> (*CP*, 189)

The poem's immediate target is the Censorship Act of 1929, but the attack hinges on comparing the twentieth-century Irish clergy who supported censorship with the eighteenth-century British government that enforced the Penal Laws. The "hedge-school" of line two refers both to the religious classes and services held in secret by Catholics during the days of the Penal Laws, and to the secret places where lovers meet to "learn by heart" what the modern Irish clergy try to "banish from the mind." The last line combines the images of people bowing their heads in prayer and of lovers joining hands and leaning toward each other behind a hedge. The title is charged with the same double meaning, referring to the Penal Laws and the Censorship Act. It also refers, through a play on "penile," to the laws of human nature and love.[7]

Clarke does not, however, settle for the confident assertion that "lovers will find / A hedge-school for themselves" and "learn by heart" all that love has to teach; he knows far too well that the church's doctrines cannot be overturned so easily. The poem that follows "Penal Law," entitled "Her Voice Could Not Be Softer," makes this point, and the two poems should be read together:

> Suddenly in the dark wood
> She turned from my arms and cried
> As if her soul were lost,
> And O too late I knew,
> Although the blame was mine,
> Her voice could not be softer
> When she told it in confession.
>
> (*CP*, 189)

Just as Clarke moved from a distant view of the "white Culdees" praying on their barren island in "Pilgrimage" to the point of view of one of the hermits in the following poem, "Celibacy," so here he shifts from the general statement made in "Penal Law" to the point of view of a young lover behind a hedge. Seen from this perspective, the question is not so simple. The lovers cannot really escape the influence of the church; the girl turns away from her lover because she cannot help seeing their lovemaking as the church would see it—that is, as a sin.

Clarke's handling of point of view is, perhaps, most successful in "Martha Blake," which manipulates the reader's perspective to enable him to see both sides of the conflict between religious doctrine and a humanistic faith in man's freedom. From the point of view of the poem's protagonist, Martha Blake, religion is seen as meeting genuine spiritual needs, but from a more distanced perspective that the poem also offers, it appears as a deceitful means of experiencing vicariously the secular pleasures that it would prohibit. At times, as in the first stanza, the poem presents both points of view simultaneously:

> Before the day is everywhere
> And the timid warmth of sleep
> Is delicate on limb, she dares
> The silence of the street

> Until the double bells are thrown back
> For Mass and echoes bound
> In the chapel yard, O then her soul
> Makes bold in the arms of sound.
>
> (*CP*, 184)

Donald Davie has pointed out how the cadence of this stanza functions expressively: "Here the 'pain'—to the reader's inner ear—comes in the fifth line, where the extra syllable at the end, 'back,' disturbs cruelly the expectation of easy pleasure built up through the liquid three/four time of the lines that precede it, and unsettles the otherwise very rich pleasure of the lines that follow, bringing the positively plummy bell-note of the perfect rhyme, 'sound / bound.' "[8] The final rhyme underscores the erotic nature of Martha's religious feelings, hinted at in the love imagery of the last line, and suggests that those emotions give the same kind of satisfaction that human love can provide. But the "pain" that Davie finds in the cadence helps the reader also see Martha from a different point of view, one intimating that Martha's religious experience is vicarious, something that causes her to turn away from the sensual reality of "the timid warmth of sleep" that is "delicate on limb."

The poem shifts to this distanced perspective in the second stanza:

> But in the shadow of the nave
> Her well-taught knees are humble,
> She does not see through any saint
> That stands in the sun
> With veins of lead, with painful crown;
> She waits that dreaded coming,
> When all the congregation bows
> And none may look up.
>
> (*CP*, 184)

Here Martha's religion, far from meeting spiritual needs, oppresses and blinds her. She prays on "well-taught knees," and is unable to "see through" the worship of religious figures represented in stained-glass windows. (The assonantal link between "veins" and "*pain*ful" emphasizes the oppressive nature of these icons.) The high point of the Mass, transubstantiation, is described as a moment when "none may look up."

When Martha takes communion, the point of view returns to her:

> The word is said, the Word sent down,
> The miracle is done
> Beneath those hands that have been rounded
> Over the embodied cup,
> And with a few, she leaves her place
> Kept by an east-filled window
> And kneels at the communion rail
> Starching beneath her chin.
>
> She trembles for the Son of Man,
> While the priest is murmuring
> What she can scarcely tell, her heart
> Is making such a stir;
> But when he picks a particle
> And she puts out her tongue,
> That joy is glittering of candles
> And benediction sung.
>
> <div align="right">(<i>CP</i>, 184)</div>

Martha is not being mocked here; the lines express a genuine response on her part, and indeed could have been written, as Davie says, "only by a poet who had experienced the Eucharist very fervently."[9] The final rhyme rounds out the stanza, suggesting, as did the rhyme between "sound" and "bound" in stanza one, the fullness of Martha's experience. The poem's perspective does not, however, stay with Martha. Indeed, it begins to slide away in the next two stanzas:

> Her soul is lying in the Presence
> Until her senses, one
> By one, desiring to attend her,
> Come as for feast and run
> So fast to share the sacrament,
> Her mouth must mother them:
> 'Sweet tooth grow wise, lip, gum be gentle,
> I touch a purple hem.'
>
> Afflicted by that love she turns
> To multiply her praise,

> Goes over all the foolish words
> And finds they are the same;
> But now she feels within her breast
> Such calm that she is silent,
> For soul can never be immodest
> Where body may not listen.
>
> (*CP*, 185)

The exaggeratedly erotic nature of the end of the first of these stanzas suggests that, for Martha, taking communion may be a vicarious means of experiencing sexual pleasures that her religious faith would deny her. The second stanza questions Martha's religious feelings partly through the double-edged "afflicted" and the pain to the reader's ear of the anagram ("silent" and "listen") that replaces the assonance or rhyme used elsewhere to close stanzas.

The final stanza allows the reader to see Martha from both perspectives:

> So to begin the common day
> She needs a miracle,
> Knowing the safety of angels
> That see her home again,
> Yet ignorant of all the rest,
> The hidden grace that people
> Hurrying to business
> Look after in the street.
>
> (*CP*, 185)

From one point of view, Martha's miracle seems merely a crutch that keeps her from seeing "the hidden grace" of human life, something to be found not in the darkness of a church but in the light of man's "business / . . . in the street." But these lines also can be read to support the point of view associated with Martha throughout the poem; it may be that Martha, not the people in the street, has the hidden grace. Although she does not realize that her sense of fulfillment is visible (she is "ignorant of all the rest"), people in the street notice it and "look after" it as they hurry to the meaningless world of their daily business.[10] Partly because of this double perspective, "Martha Blake" does more than counsel outright rejection of religious faith. It also suggests, as does "Tenebrae," that religious belief, however irreconcilable with reason, cannot be wholly set aside, because it, and not reason, recognizes man's spiritual needs. The result is, as it was at the end of "Tenebrae," a state of limbo.

In its use of a persona, "Martha Blake" differs from most of the poems in *Night and Morning*, which are confessional. One of the most impressive of Clarke's poems, "The Straying Student," also relies on a persona, a variation of the wayward scholar found in Clarke's first play, *The Son of Learning*. In addition, this poem combines the flesh-spirit conflict of *Pilgrimage* and the reason-religion dichotomy of *Night and Morning* in a comprehensive assertion of Clarke's humanism:

> On a holy day when sails were blowing southward,
> A bishop sang the Mass at Inishmore,
> Men took one side, their wives were on the other
> But I heard the woman coming from the shore:
> And wild in despair my parents cried aloud
> For they saw the vision draw me to the doorway.
>
> Long had she lived in Rome when Popes were bad,
> The wealth of every age she makes her own,
> Yet smiled on me in eager admiration,
> And for a summer taught me all I know,
> Banishing shame with her great laugh that rang
> As if a pillar caught it back alone.
>
> I learned the prouder counsel of her throat,
> My mind was growing bold as light in Greece;
> And when in sleep her stirring limbs were shown,
> I blessed the noonday rock that knew no tree:
> And for an hour the mountain was her throne,
> Although her eyes were bright with mockery.
>
> They say I was sent back from Salamanca
> And failed in logic, but I wrote her praise
> Nine times upon a college wall in France.
> She laid her hand at darkfall on my page
> That I might read the heavens in a glance
> And I knew every star the Moors have named.
>
> Awake or in my sleep, I have no peace now,
> Before the ball is struck, my breath has gone,

And yet I tremble lest she may deceive me
And leave me in this land, where every woman's son
Must carry his own coffin and believe,
In dread, all that the clergy teach the young.

(*CP*, 188–189)

The style of "The Straying Student," as well as its use of a persona, distinguishes it from most of *Night and Morning*; its smooth and erotic rhythms, frequent similes and metaphors, and, above all, complex patterns of assonance make it as melodious a poem as Clarke ever wrote. It is built around an *abbac* pattern of internal assonance, sounded on the five stressed syllables of each line:

a b b a c
On a *holy day* when *sails* were *blow*ing *south*ward.

There are, of course, variations, as in the third line:

a b b c d
Men *took* one *side*, their *wives* were *on* the *oth*er,

or as in this line from stanza two:

a a b b c
The *wealth* of *every age* she *makes* her *own*.

Clarke also uses cross-rhyming between words in terminal positions—in stanza one, "Inish*more*," "shore," and "*door*way" (Augustine Martin has pointed out how the "o" sound moves back along the word in this progression, muting "the crude clapper of rhyme"[11])—as well as cross-assonance: "*south*ward" and "*a*loud." In addition, assonance links words in terminal positions with words in medial positions; in the first stanza, "*holy*" and "*blow*ing" find an echo in "Inish*more*," and the second syllable of "doorway" echoes "de*spair*" and "*par*ents."[12]

This music often functions expressively. In the last line of stanza one, the pattern of internal assonance sounded in the first five lines is replaced by an internal rhyme between "saw" and "draw," echoing the connection between what the student sees and what he does. The poem's entire range of sound patterns begins to fade near the end, especially in the last stanza; Clarke said that he deliberately broke up the pattern to reflect the doubt and despair with which the poem concludes.[13]

The woman who leads the student out of church and away from his religious upbringing represents the importance of sexuality and human love (as do the young woman of Beare and Queen Gormlai) and intellectual and artistic freedom—in short, everything that Clarke believes in and sees the Irish Catholic Church as opposed to. That opposition appears in the first line of the poem, which sets up a tension between the church's demands for attendance at mass on holy days of obligation and the image of blowing sails, suggesting an alluring natural beauty lying outside the purview of the church. The woman who tempts the student comes from the natural world, and her arrival is marked by a change from the conventional iambic movement of line three, divided by a caesura that reinforces the historically accurate description of the church as divided according to sex, to a line that begins with an anapaestic foot and flows to its conclusion without interruption: "But I heard the woman coming from the shore."

The middle three stanzas describe the student's experience, whether real or visionary, as he moves away from his religious beliefs and toward the humanism that the woman represents. The woman challenges both the guilt that the church has associated with the enjoyment of sexuality ("banishing shame with her great laugh that rang"), and the church's disapproving attitude toward reason. The "prouder counsel of her throat" combines the two, referring to the woman's physical beauty and to her words, which make the student's mind grow "bold as light in Greece." This phrase picks up the dark-light imagery that runs through much of *Night and Morning*, and alludes to the "light" of Greek philosophy, which honored mind and body, and which lies at the source of the humanistic tradition. In the fourth stanza (described by Augustine Martin as "surely one of the most splendid stanzas in Irish poetry"[14]), the "logic" of religious discipline and thinking is rejected for an art inspired by the humanistic values of the woman ("she laid her hand at darkfall on my page") and by an instinctual, even visionary knowledge that ignores religious restrictions on reason; the student learns to "read the heavens with a glance" (instead of aspiring to the single remote heaven of his religion), and to see from a radically different, non-Christian point of view ("and I knew every star the Moors have named").

The world of religious prohibition is not, however, simply erased from the student's consciousness. For one thing, as the last stanza makes clear, the great force of the church in Ireland is still to be reckoned with. But there is another reason for the student's dread at the end of the poem. His experience with the woman has exploded the religious doctrines that he was brought up on, but nothing that he has learned from her is itself free from doubt. The student's mortality, the coffin that he must carry with him, reminds him that all his newly won freedom ignores the possibility, central to the church's teachings, that life may go on beyond the grave. And so the student is left facing precisely what Clarke confronts throughout *Night and Morning*: uncertainty, fear of death, and spiritual despair—in short, the "Darkness that man must dread at last."

No study of Clarke's "Court of Judgment" poetry is complete without a consideration of "Ancient Lights." Although this poem did not appear until 1955, seventeen years after *Night and Morning* and twenty-six after *Pilgrimage*, it deals with the major conflicts central to these two volumes. In fact, the poem's relatively late appearance in Clarke's canon makes it all the more significant. Several critics have seen "Ancient Lights" as a pivotal poem describing a resolution of the fundamental tensions informing Clarke's earlier work, and enabling him to turn to the public poetry that he began writing in the 1950s.[15]

Without doubt, the volume *Ancient Lights* marks a new phase in Clarke's career, and it is plausible enough to see the title poem as a transition between intensely personal poems like "Tenebrae" and the later public poems. But to argue that it settles the conflicts described in *Pilgrimage* and *Night and Morning* is to see Clarke as suddenly getting free of a spiritual dilemma that, as he insisted again and again, cannot be escaped. Also, to hold such a view is to risk misreading much of Clarke's later work, including many of the public poems that supposedly depend on a resolution of the conflicts expressed in the earlier work. "Ancient Lights" describes a moment of spiritual release with impressive force and conviction, but it is only a moment. That moment cannot release Clarke, however much he may have wanted it to (or, by placing the poem where he did, have wanted his readers to think that it could), from either the struggle between his religious upbringing and his embracing of humanism, or from the spiritual despair engendered by his attempts to reconcile the two.

The poem opens with the familiar contrast between day and night, between the world of humanism and that of religion:

When all of us wore smaller shoes
And knew the next world better than
The knots we broke, I used to hurry
On missions of my own to Capel
Street, Bolton Street and Granby Row
To see what man has made. But darkness
Was roomed with fears. Sleep, stripped by woes
I had been taught, beat door, leaped landing,
Lied down the bannisters of naught.

(CP, 199)

The speaker's efforts to know man's world are countered here by the blinding force of his religion. The image of sleep being interrupted by the fears and guilt generated by his religious training ("the woes / I had been taught") recalls several passages from *Night and Morning*: "I know the injured pride of sleep" ("Night and Morning"), "When I was younger than the soul / That wakes me now at night" ("Repentence"), and "When sleep has shot the bolt and bar, / And reason fails at midnight" ("Summer Lightning").

The poem then shifts to a specific part of Clarke's religious upbringing, his terrifying experience in the confessional:

Being sent to penance, come Saturday,
I shuffled slower than my sins should.
My fears were candle-spiked at side-shrines,
Rays lengthened them in stained-glass. Confided
To night again, my grief bowed down,
Heard hand on shutter-knob. Did I
Take pleasure, when alone—how much—
In a bad thought, immodest look
Or worse, unnecessary touch?

Closeted in the confessional,
I put on flesh, so many years
Were added to my own, attempted
In vain to keep Dominican
As much i' the dark as I was, mixing
Whispered replies with his low words;
Then shuddered past the crucifix,
The feet so hammered, daubed-on blood-drip,
Black with lip-scrimmage of the damned.

(CP, 199)

In *Twice Round the Black Church*, Clarke recalls one specific Satur-
day that resembles the experience described in these stanzas:

> Soon compulsory confession was to become a weekly ordeal.
> Obscurely, through the grille, came warnings against curiosity, body-
> blighting sins, voluntary emissions that would eventually bring on
> madness. . . . For some time after I became ashamed to confess my
> sins to Father O'Hara, I discovered by chance that Father Gough,
> though gruff in his manner, was very hard of hearing. One Saturday, I
> had an unusually large burden of bad thoughts: being truthful, I had
> tried to count them as they flitted in and out of my mind. The choleric
> old man must have caught my faint whisper for he exclaimed, "How
> many times did you say?" "Forty times, Father." "Get out of me box,
> yeh young blaggard." I crept out, shame-faced, fearing that the other
> penitents had heard his angry words. It was getting late and I was faced
> once more with the problem of returning home in a state of grace.
> There was only one hope left on earth—the gentle Father O'Hara who
> knew so well all the sufferings of the young. I hurried over to the "Poor
> Side" of the chapel, passed the Figure of the Crucifix, the nailed feet
> black with the kisses of the people. . . . I was the last sinner and Father
> O'Hara had already taken off his stole. He put it on again, listened
> patiently to my confused explanation. "Did you take pleasure in these
> thoughts?" "Yes, Father." "Did you. . ." He hesitated and his voice was
> almost a sigh. "Did you let your nature flow?" "No, Father." I heard
> once more the sound of the soul-washing Latin and I hurried home-
> ward, safe for a few more days from the torments of the world below.[16]

In the poem, despite the humorous account of the young Clarke
trying "to keep Dominican / As much i' the dark as I was," the full
terror of the experience comes across, partly through references that
echo the atmosphere of darkness and confinement created in *Night
and Morning*, and partly through the descriptions of religious icons in
the church. The side-altar candles and stained-glass windows sym-
bolize not God's glory, but man's shame: "My fears were candle-
spiked at side-shrines, / Rays lengthened them in stained-glass." The
crucifix is seen as especially grotesque, blackened with signs of man's
corruption, "lip-scrimmage of the damned."

The moment of spiritual release that the poem celebrates begins in the next stanza, which moves from the darkness and closeness of the confession box to the light and openness of the outside:

> Once as I crept from the church-steps,
> Beside myself, the air opened
> On purpose. Nature read in a flutter
> An evening lesson above my head.
> Atwirl beyond the leadings, corbels,
> A cage-bird came among sparrows
> (The moral inescapable)
> Plucked, roof-mired, all in mad bits. O
> The pizzicato of its wires!
>
>   (*CP*, 199–200)

The lesson that Nature reads here is the celebration of natural life, including sexual pleasure, for which the speaker has just been made to feel such guilt in the confessional. The narrator sees himself as a "cage-bird," stripped of his natural instincts, mired to the teachings of his religion, and profoundly unsettled. (Clarke did, in fact, spend thirteen months in a mental institution as a young man.) This bird emerges suddenly, coming "among sparrows" to catch a glimpse of freedom.

The poem concludes with a moment of vision in which the speaker, like the caged bird, experiences a sudden release from the oppression and darkness of religious stricture:

> Still, still I remember awful downpour
> Cabbing Mountjoy Street, spun loneliness
> Veiling almost the Protestant church,
> Two backyards from my very home,
> I dared to shelter at locked door.
> There, walled by heresy, my fears
> Were solved. I had absolved myself:
> Feast-day effulgence, as though I gained
> For life a plenary indulgence.
>
> The sun came out, new smoke flew up,
> The gutters of the Black Church rang
> With services. Waste water mocked
> The ballcocks: down-pipes sparrowing,

And all around the spires of Dublin
Such swallowing in the air, such cowling
To keep high offices pure: I heard
From shore to shore, the iron gratings
Take half our heavens with a roar.
                    (*CP*, 200–201)

The revelation occurs in the doorway of the Protestant "Black Church" near Clarke's boyhood home—a private symbol for the shadow that his own religion cast across his life. Significantly, the epiphany is described in terms taken from that religion. In the first stanza, Clarke transforms the Catholic doctrines of absolution and plenary indulgence (in which special prayers and devotions remit the temporal punishment that is part of the penalty of sin) into a remission of the church's doctrines and teachings that frees him "for life." The phrase "plenary indulgence" also suggests that Clarke can now indulge in the pleasures of life, sensual and intellectual.

In the last stanza, the sacrament of penace, which darkened the early stanzas, gives way to a secular baptism. As the religious ritual of baptism is said to cleanse man of Original Sin, the rainwater from the storm washes away the guilt and fear associated with Clarke's religious upbringing. The great verbal energy of the final stanza reflects the action of the life-giving rainwater. The echoes between "up" and "*gut*ter," "mocked" and "ball*cocks*," and "*cowl*ing" and "*swal*lowing"; the images of "down-pipes sparrowing" (recalling the symbolic sparrows of the fourth stanza), of "such swallowing in the air" (another suggestion of freedom), and of "cowling / To keep high offices pure" (picturing the wind as cleansing the air even as it turns the cowls on rooftop ventilation shafts and chimneys); and the skillful control of iambic rhythms (the great force of "rang" at the end of line two, for example) add up to a description that powerfully imitates the sense of sudden release being described.[17] In the end, the church and all its "darkness / . . . roomed with fears" is, for the moment anyway, drowned in the onomatopoeic "roar" that rings the poem to its conclusion.

But exactly how much is sluiced away in that final roar of rainwater? One might note that those iron gratings take but "half our heavens with a roar," leaving, presumably, another half somewhere beyond their power. One might also recall that seventeen years earlier, Clarke published a poem in which the bright sun of reason was described as making "a show / Of half the world." And finally, conscious of the religious imagery that runs through all these "Court of Judgment" poems, from the first stanza of "Pilgrimage" to the last of "Ancient Lights," one might remember the comment that was made to Stephen Dedalus in the novel of another twentieth-century Irish Catholic trying to fly past the nets of his religion: "It is a curious thing, do you know, Cranly said dispassionately, how your mind is super-saturated with the religion in which you say you disbelieve."[18]

5

"The World's Mad Business" (I):
Shorter Public Poems

Clarke left Ireland in 1922, the year when the Irish Civil War began and certainly the most divisive of all the troubled years that followed the Easter Rising. Clarke's personal and professional life was also extremely troubled at this time; his first marriage had failed, and his teaching contract at University College, Dublin, had not been renewed. Nonetheless, Clarke departed with considerable reluctance. "Being restless and still disturbed by the failure of my secular marriage, I decided to go back to London," he writes in *Twice Round the Black Church*. "I did so with regret for, despite the emotional havoc of the Civil War and its immediate miseries, the Irish Free State was just beginning and hopes for a small independent literature with its own standards of criticism were astir."[1]

Clarke stayed in England for fifteen years; when he returned to Ireland to live, settling into the roomy stone house that his mother had acquired for him on the River Dodder in Templeogue, most of the turbulence, public and private, that he had left behind in 1922 had passed. But the Ireland of 1937 held, in Clarke's view, much less promise than the Ireland of 1922. The revolutionary fervor of the Rising and its aftermath had been replaced by a complacent, middle-class political conservatism; the literary revival that had inspired Clarke in his youth was dead in letter and spirit, leaving in its wake a group of disaffected writers working under the shadow of a repressive Censorship Act; and the Irish Catholic Church that had come to stand, in Clarke's mind, for everything opposed to man's spiritual, intellectual, and moral freedom had risen to a position of power and influence undreamt of a century earlier.

Clarke's reaction to all this took him out of the private world of *Night and Morning* and into the public arena of the theatre and, later, of a radically different kind of poetry—the satirical poems and epigrams that make up the bulk of his work in the 1950s and 1960s. Clarke threw himself into the theatre shortly after his return to Ireland; he set up a verse-speaking society and later the Lyric Theatre, and also began writing verse plays that were often thinly veiled attacks on the Catholic Church. With the appearance of *Ancient Lights* in 1955, Clarke returned, after an eighteen-year hiatus, to writing poetry—not the private poetry of *Pilgrimage* and *Night and Morning*, but a very different public poetry that made pointed and wide-ranging attacks on all phases of modern Irish life. For the next thirteen years, in everything from stinging epigrams to long, semi-meditative poems, Clarke poured out his frustrations and anger against an Ireland that he saw as a church-dominated society in which individual freedom was thwarted, social justice was ignored, and idealism, especially the nationalistic idealism that Clarke associated with the Easter Rising, was perverted.

During these years, Clarke's reputation outside Ireland, which had languished after the early success of *The Vengeance of Fionn*, began suddenly to flourish. The publication in England and the United States of *Later Poems* (1961), which brought together the poems of *Pilgrimage* and *Night and Morning* with those of *Ancient Lights* and the two volumes of satirical verse that followed it, made Clarke's work available, for the first time, to a wide audience. The growth of Clarke's reputation during the next few years proved, however, something of a mixed blessing. Because *Later Poems* consisted mostly of satirical verse, and because the majority of poems that Clarke published in the 1960s were attacks on specific aspects of modern Irish society, Clarke became known principally as an Irish satirist whose appeal was limited to readers interested in contemporary Irish affairs or willing to take on the considerable work required to meet Clarke on his own ground. And so it became easy to read Clarke—and, in some instances, to dismiss him—as a provincial writer.

This view does a serious disservice to Clarke's work as a satirist.

It also overlooks the important connection between Clarke's satirical verse and the poems of *Pilgrimage* and *Night and Morning*. The private struggle documented in these two volumes between Clarke's Irish Catholic upbringing and his faith in essentially humanistic values is not simply abandoned in Clarke's later work; rather, his satirical poems represent a transformation of a private debate into a public quarrel. In criticizing the institutional and often alarmingly political manifestations of the Catholic Church in Ireland, these poems carry on Clarke's war against religious attitudes that would deny man his right to freedom, private or public. And it is precisely this dimension of Clarke's public poetry that raises it above the category of provincial satire.

Clarke's public poetry can be divided into two parts. The first consists of the shorter poems and epigrams that comment, usually quite specifically and often as occasional verse, on the political and religious climate of modern Ireland. These poems, which began appearing in *Ancient Lights*, represent a significant portion of Clarke's work through *A Sermon on Swift* in 1968. The second category (discussed in the next chapter) consists of a number of relatively long poems, written during the same period, that combine public comment with private memory. These poems offer the same vision of a church-dominated and destructively conservative Ireland that informs the shorter public poems, but they also attack aspects of modern Ireland familiar to most western nations in the twentieth century—the spread of suburban development, for example, and the destruction of the natural environment. Moreover, largely through the personal voice that distinguishes them from Clarke's other public poetry, these poems also question the assumptions that lie behind these developments: the notion that material gain and "progress" are of overriding importance, and the concurrent rejection of less tangible, but more humanistic values, especially human love.

The first poem in *Ancient Lights*, "Celebrations," is fairly typical of the poetry in the first of these two categories. It is heavily ironic, its language is dense and often deliberately ambivalent, and it is an occasional and extremely specific poem. (It was first published in 1941, the year of the twenty-fifth anniversary of the Easter Rising, and refers to the Dublin Eucharistic Congress of 1932.[2]) It is also bitterly critical of the "new Ireland":

Who dare complain or be ashamed
Of liberties our arms have taken?
For every spike upon that gateway,
We have uncrowned the past:
And open hearts are celebrating
Prosperity of church and state
In the shade of Dublin Castle.

So many flagpoles can be seen now
Freeing the crowd, while crisscross keys,
On yellow-and-white above the green,
Treble the wards of nation,
God only knows what treasury
Uncrams to keep each city borough
And thoroughfare in grace.

Let ageing politicians pray
Again, hoardings recount our faith,
The blindfold woman in a rage
Condemn her own for treason:
No steeple topped the scale that Monday,
Rebel souls had lost their savings
And looters braved the street.

(*CP*, 195)

In his public poetry, Clarke tends to use ambiguity for ironic effect. The question that opens the poem, for example, appears at first glance to be rhetorical, but it also suggests, partly because of the ambiguity of "dare," that no one can risk complaint in a society where freedom of speech is sharply curtailed. Similarly, the two following lines seem to celebrate Ireland's success in driving Britain out of the larger part of Ireland, but they also intimate—if "every spike upon that gateway" is taken to refer not to Irish heads impaled by the British on the gateway to Dublin Castle, but to the heads of Irish Republicans executed by post-Treaty governments—that in exchanging British domination for the rule of such men, the Irish have lost something valuable, something worth being crowned: a past in which the true spirit of nationalism flourished.[3] The last three lines of the first stanza are more overtly ironic, emphasizing that what is being celebrated at the Eucharistic Conference is the material "prosperity" of church and state (yoked together in the line as they are in fact).

The notion hinted at in the last line of the first stanza—that the Irish have gained very little, if any, freedom in driving out the British—is carried forward, again largely through irony, in the second stanza. The Irish are seen here as owing allegiance not just to the British but to "so many flagpoles": that of the church, symbolized by the papal flag ("crisscross keys, / On yellow-and-white"); that of the British, referred to in "above the green," an allusion to College Green, the site of that bastion of British influence in Ireland, Trinity College; and that of the Irish government itself. The power of the church in this alliance is singled out in the ironic assertion that "God only knows" what the government is spending to keep the city "in grace."

Having railed at the materialism of church and state, and at the efforts of those institutions to subvert Irish liberty, the poem turns in the final stanza to direct invective and to a devastating comparison of the Ireland being celebrated at the Eucharistic Congress to the Ireland of the Easter Rising. In the new Ireland, politicians are chained to the church ("Let ageing politicians pray"), the church is blatantly materialistic ("hoardings recount our faith"), and the government, in executing Republican extremists, has betrayed both a sense of justice and the spirit of Irish nationalism ("The blindfold woman in a rage / Condemn her own for treason"). In contrast, the second half of the stanza argues that the men who led the Rising were not controlled by the church, which had, in fact, opposed the Republican movement ("No steeple topped the scale that Monday"—both in the sense of a steeple symbolically crowning the city's skyline and of the church tipping the scales of justice). It also insists that the rebels were motivated by idealism, not the sordid materialism of the modern church and state; they lost, willingly, their "savings"—their material goods and comforts, but also, for some, their lives, and, insofar as they believed that their actions violated the teachings of their religious faith, their souls. In the end, what the poem most admires about the Rising is the idealism and belief in freedom that motivated it; what it most detests about modern Ireland is the materialism and denial of freedom that, in Clarke's view, motivate it. Thus, "Celebrations" does more than attack the new Ireland; it also makes a specific and forceful argument for the importance of idealism and human freedom.

Another poem in *Ancient Lights* structured around a contrast

between the days of the Easter Rising and those that succeeded it is
"Inscription for a Headstone." The poem's immediate subject is the
Irish labor leader James Larkin and "Bloody Sunday," the day in 1913
when police charged a crowd gathered in O'Connell Street to hear
Larkin deliver an illegal speech during the Great Lockout:

> What Larkin bawled to hungry crowds
> Is murmured now in dining-hall
> And study. Faith bestirs itself
> Lest infidels in their impatience
> Leave it behind. Who could have guessed
> Batons were blessings in disguise,
> When every ambulance was filled
> With half-killed men and Sunday trampled
> Upon unrest? Such fear can harden
> Or soften heart, knowing too clearly
> His name endures on our holiest page,
> Scrawled in a rage by Dublin's poor.
>
> (*CP*, 202)

Larkin's fiery socialism had once posed a serious threat to the Irish
Catholic Church, and the church fought Larkin and his campaign
passionately; but now, the opening lines suggest, the danger is gone,
and socialism is safe enough for seminary discussions among well-fed
and passive clerics and even for politically necessary gestures of
support. This emasculation of socialistic ideals is insisted on in the
contrast between "bawled" and "murmured" and between "hungry
crowds" and "dining-hall." The poem also connects the church to the
violent repression of workers on Bloody Sunday. The Sunday of
"Sunday trampled / Upon unrest" refers to the church as well as the
event, suggesting that because of its militant opposition to Larkin, the
church can be held responsible for condoning the violence used to put
down the demonstration. Thus, the church emerges as a champion of
a vicious anti-humanism that would deny the human rights that
Larkin was fighting for, and approve the inhumane and un-Christian
methods used to suppress them. This dimension of the poem's attack
on the church is developed in the closing lines, primarily by means of
a religious metaphor. Larkin's name and what he fought for will last,
these lines insist, because they speak for something that is sacred—
not as defined by a church that is opposed to humanistic values, but as

defined by a humanism that honors man and his fundamental rights.

"Inscription for a Headstone" also provides an example of the stylistic achievements of Clarke's public verse. The same craftsmanship that resulted in the rich assonantal poems of *Pilgrimage* and *Night and Morning* is at work here to produce a far different quality, but one that reinforces the poem's assertions. Assonance and rhyme connect each pair of lines in a pattern linking terminal with medial words:

> What Larkin bawled to hungry crowds
> Is murmured now in dining hall.

This pattern continues throughout the poem, and, in addition to underscoring important words like "bawled," "blessings," and "heart," organizes the poem into six couplets. But frequent runovers and uneven rhythms violate this organization, creating a deliberately irritating tension that reflects the physical violence of Bloody Sunday and the moral violence that the Irish Catholic Church is being charged with.

The same kind of calculated roughness can be found in another early satirical poem, "The Trial of Robert Emmet" (*Too Great a Vine*, 1957). This poem was inspired by a plan, eventually scrapped, to reenact the trial of the Irish patriot Robert Emmet, executed in 1803 for his part in an abortive rising:

> Sentence the lot and hurry them away,
> The court must now be cleared, batten and spot
> Swung up with rope and ladder, lighting-plot
> Rehearsed. No need of drop-scene for the play
> Tonight: bench, box and bar in well-mixed ray
> Make do. Though countless miscreants have got
> A life-term here, and some, the scaffold knot,
> Forget the cells our safety fills by day.
> See British greed and tyranny defied
> Once more by that freethinker in the dock
> And sigh because his epitaph remains
> Unwritten. Cheer revolution by the clock
> And lastly—badge and holy medal guide
> Your cars home, hooting through our dirtiest lanes.
>
> (*CP*, 208)

Here Clarke uses awkward runovers and disruptive rhythms to upset the implicit symmetry of the sonnet. This twisting of the sonnet into something ungainly mirrors the poem's argument that the spirit of Irish nationalism has been perverted into a romantic chauvinism that obscures pressing human and social needs. The octet compares the plans for the reenactment of Emmet's trial with the treatment given by de Valera's government to Republican diehards, something that Clarke attacked in "Celebrations." Both actions, the poem suggests, betray nationalistic ideals, making a mockery of what Emmet stood for. They also betray something more fundamental; the last line of the octet questions not only the treatment of Republican intransigents but also the morally bankrupt point of view that is willing to ignore or condone injustice for selfish ends. The human cost of this attitude is counted in the sestet. The kind of nationalism behind the plan for a mock trial is seen as foolishly romantic ("And *sigh* because his epitaph remains / Unwritten") and safely distanced, like a spectator sport or entertainment that calls for no commitment. The result is anything but benign, as the final two lines of the poem insist. Imagining the crowd on its way home from the mock trial, Clarke sees the Irish as lulled by a shallow nationalism and the false comfort of their religion into turning their backs on the social needs of fellow human beings. "Hooting" expresses precisely the kind of anti-humanistic attitude that the poem is attacking, one not by any means limited to the Irish.

In *Twice Round the Black Church*, Clarke makes a comment that bears significantly on his public poetry: "It takes us many years to learn that the passion for justice and the welfare of all, once it has been aroused, is the deepest one in mortal life."[4] For Clarke, the most potent force working against that passion in modern Ireland is the Catholic Church. "St. Christopher," an epigram that closes *Too Great a Vine*, might be set alongside Clarke's statement about social justice and welfare:

> Child that his strength upbore,
> Knotted as tree-trunks i' the spate,
> Became a giant, whose weight
> Unearthed the river from shore
> Till saint's bones were a-crack.
> Fabulist, can an ill state
> Like ours, carry so great
> A Church upon its back?

(*CP*, 219)

Clarke's career as a public poet can be seen largely as an attempt to answer that final question with a resounding "no," and a significant portion of his satirical verse is directed specifically at the Catholic Church and its influence.

In 1951, the church helped defeat a controversial "mother-and-child" proposal, calling for free health care for children under sixteen and for free maternity care; the church saw the plan as a threat to the sanctity of the family, guaranteed in no less authoritative a document than the 1937 Constitution, and as something that could lead to unmonitored sex education. Clarke responded to the church's intervention with "Mother and Child" (*Ancient Lights*). The poem points to the 1951 general election, in which the coalition government that had introduced the plan was beaten, as evidence of the church's corruptive influence:

> Obedient keys rattled in locks,
> Bottles in old dispensaries
> Were shaken and the ballot boxes
> Hid politicians on their knees
> When pity showed us what we are.
> 'Why should we care,' votes cried, 'for child
> Or mother? Common help is harmful
> And state-control must starve the soul.'
> One doctor spoke out. Bishops mitred.
> But now our caution has been mended,
> The side-door opened, bill amended.
> We profit from God's love and pity,
> Sampling the world with good example.
> Before you damp it with your spit,
> Respect our newest postage stamp.
>
> (*CP*, 202)

The image of ballot boxes hiding "politicians on their knees" is central to Clarke's vision of modern Ireland, and the effect of the church's conservative influence is, in Clarke's view, social injustice. The church's argument that the "mother-and-child" proposal would destroy the sanctity of the family ("state-control must starve the soul"—where the internal rhyme adds a mocking note) is seen as promoting the anti-humanistic and un-Christian attitude of neglect: "Why should we care . . . for child / Or mother?" The destructive

hypocrisy behind the church's position, which, in the name of pro-
tecting the maternal relationship, would make it more difficult for
many women to be good mothers, is brought home in the final ironic
illusion to a government-issued stamp picturing the Madonna and
child. (The poem is subtitled "Marian Year Stamp: 1954.")

When Douglas Hyde, the poet and Gaelic scholar who had
fought to revive the Irish language and who later became the first
president of Ireland under the 1937 Constitution, was buried, Clarke
found another occasion to ridicule "politicians on their knees." In
"Burial of an Irish President" (*Flight to Africa*, 1963), Clarke describes
the scene inside St. Patrick's Cathedral, the Protestant church where
funeral services for Hyde were held, and then shifts to what was
happening outside:

> . . . Outside
> The hush of Dublin town,
> Professors of cap and gown,
> Costello, his Cabinet,
> In Government cars, hiding
> Around the corner, ready
> Tall hat in hand, dreading
> *Our Father* in English. Better
> Not hear that 'which' for 'who'
> And risk eternal doom.
>
> (*CP*, 250)

The amusing picture of Ireland's political leaders afraid to violate the
Catholic Church's taboo on attending non-Catholic services, even to
honor one of the country's most respected figures, points to the
slavish dependence of Irish politicians on the church, and to the
religious bigotry that the church's doctrine promotes. The pettiness
of the church's attitude toward Protestantism is emphasized in the
mocking description at the end of the poem of the slight difference
between the Protestant and Catholic versions of the Lord's Prayer.

A more complex and far-reaching poem about religious bigotry is
"Street Game" (*Flight to Africa*):

> Unholy bits, ring, neck, of porter and Bass bottle
> From the six public-houses at those four corners,
> Nicholas St, Clanbrassil St, the Coombe
> And Kevin St, shrine on high wall—fierce spot—

Protecting the Sisters of the Holy Faith, warning
By sun and moon the ruffians in top-back room
Or cellar. Last week I saw a marching band,
Small Protestants in grey clothes, well-fed pairs
Led by a Bible teacher, heard the noise
Of boot-heel metal by bread-shop, sweet-shop, dairy,
Scrap, turf, wood, coal-blocks. Suddenly Catholic joylets
Darted from alleys, raggedy cherubs that dared them:
'Luk, feckin' bastards, swaddlers, feckin' bastards!'
Too well they knew the words their mothers, fathers,
Used. Silent, the foundlings marched along the street-path
With clink of boot-heel metal. We have cast
Them out. Devotion, come to the man-hole at last,
Bawls: 'Feckin' bastards, swaddlers, feckin' bastards!'

(*CP*, 256)

On the surface, the poem condemns the behavior of the Catholic
children, and suggests that the hatred inspired by religious bigotry is
part of the legacy of Irish Catholicism. But the poem is more complex
than that. The Protestant orphans are described as "well-fed," in
obvious contrast to the "raggedy cherubs" living amid the squalor of
the Coombe (a poor area of Dublin). Also, the sound of "boot-heel
metal," made by the foundlings as they march along, is calculated to
call up feelings of military oppression, especially since the orphans
are Protestants and so associated, in the minds of many Irish Catholics
at least, with the Ascendancy. In trying in this way to account for the
feelings of the Catholic children, the poem moves beyond a simple
condemnation of religious bigotry among Irish Catholics to a much
broader statement about religious and political discrimination in
general.[5]

Clarke was keenly aware that the Irish Catholic Church, because
of its strictly enforced puritanical views on sex and, more specifically,
its refusal to sanction birth control, influenced the private as well as
the public lives of twentieth-century Irishmen. "The Envy of Poor
Lovers" (*Ancient Lights*) is one of several satirical poems that address
this aspect of Catholic Ireland. The poem takes the reader back to the
lovers seen behind hedges in "Penal Law" and "Her Voice Could Not
be Softer":

Pity poor lovers who may not do what they please
With their kisses under a hedge, before a raindrop
Unhouses it; and astir from wretched centuries,
Bramble and briar remind them of the saints.

Her envy is the curtain seen at night-time,
Happy position that could change her name.
His envy—clasp of the married whose thoughts can be alike,
Whose nature flows without the blame or shame.

Lying in the grass as if it were a sin
To move, they hold each other's breath, tremble,
Ready to share that ancient dread—kisses begin
Again—of Ireland keeping company with them.

Think, children, of institutions mured above
Your ignorance, where every look is veiled,
State-paid to snatch away the folly of poor lovers
For whom, it seems, the sacraments have failed.

(CP, 205)

The first three stanzas are closer to *Pilgrimage* and *Night and Morning*
than to most of Clarke's public poetry. The tension between natural
desire and the prohibitive doctrines of the church—felt especially in
the interruption of "that ancient dread . . . of Ireland keeping com-
pany with them" by "kisses begin again"—is the same dichotomy that
informs the earlier volumes. The last stanza, however, is clearly the
work of Clarke the satirist. The "institutions . . . where every look is
veiled" refer to Catholic orphanages where illegitimate children are
commonly placed, and the poem attacks this specific practice as an
example of the church's anti-humanistic attitudes. The biting, Swift-
ian irony of this stanza, particularly of the devastating "it seems,"
gives the poem the satiric edge so common to Clarke's public poetry.

"Marriage" (*Ancient Lights*) attacks the church's ban on con-
traceptives by arguing that the method of birth control forced on
Catholics, the rhythm method, casts a shadow of guilt over the
pleasures of lovemaking:

Parents are sinful now, for they must whisper
Too much in the dark. Aye, there's the rub! What grace
Can snatch the small hours from that costly kiss?

> Those who slip off the ring, try to be chaste
> And when they cannot help it, steal the crumbs
> From their own wedding breakfast, spare expense
> And keep in warmth the children they have nourished.
> But shall the sweet promise of the sacrament
> Gladden the heart, if mortals calculate
> Their pleasures by the calendar? Night-school
> Of love where all, who learn to cheat, grow pale
> With guilty hope at every change of moon!
>
> (CP, 196)

The fulfillment of natural desire and the expression of love through sexuality cannot take place, the poem insists, under the conditions of the rhythm method; sexuality and love are distinctly human qualities, and cannot be arbitrarily regulated "by the calendar." That the Irish Catholic Church fails to recognize this—or to recognize the cost to all concerned of the failure of the rhythm method—is just one more sign, in Clarke's view, of the church's anti-humanistic attitudes.

Unfortunately, Clarke's feelings about the influence of the church in modern Ireland are not always expressed with the control evident in poems like "The Envy of Poor Lovers" or "Marriage." On occasion, Clarke's bitter anger drives him into untenable positions that undermine the humanistic values that his public poetry generally argues for. An example is "Living on Sin" (*Flight to Africa*):

> The hasty sin of the young after a dance,
> Awkward in clothes against a wall or crick-necked
> In car, gives many a nun her tidy bed,
> Full board and launderette. God-fearing State
> Provides three pounds a week, our conscience money,
> For every infant severed from the breast.
>
> (CP, 271)

The satire here is derailed by the implication that the nuns who work with illegitimate children in Catholic orphanages are making a comfortable living from the sins of others (an implication furthered by the poem's title: "Living *on* Sin"). This suggestion runs so counter to reality, and ignores so cruelly the often unselfish motives of nuns in these institutions, that the poem loses its credibility, and, what is worse, is vulnerable to the charge that it is as anti-humanistic as the practice that it attacks.

Some of Clarke's public poems, especially in *Flight to Africa* and later volumes, are marred by stylistic excesses. In a number of these, the subtle control through assonance, rhythm, and syntax observable in poems like "Inscription for a Headstone" and "The Trial of Robert Emmet" gives way to a much more contrived verse, often inappropriately dependent on the ironic effects of Hudibrastic rhymes, homonyms, and *rime riche*.[6] The damage that this can cause is evident in "New Liberty Hall" (*The Echo at Coole*, 1968), which, like "Inscription for a Headstone," contrasts the present with the Ireland of James Larkin. The poem begins in a relatively light vein, mocking the hypocrisy behind the modern glass office building that replaced the grim brick Liberty Hall, headquarters for Larkin and James Connolly, and the building that Connolly led his troops out of on Easter Monday, 1916:

> Higher than county lark
> Can fly, a speck that sings,
> Sixteen-floored Liberty Hall
> Goes up through scaffoldings
> In memory of Larkin,
> Shot Connolly. With cap
> On simple head, hallmark
> Of sweat, new capitalists
> Rent out expensive suites
> Of glassier offices,
> Babel'd above our streets,
> The unemployed may scoff, but
> Workers must skimp and scrape
> To own so fine a skyscraper,
> Beyond the dream of Gandon,
> Shaming the Custom House
> The giant crane, the gantries.
>   (*CP*, 429)

The appropriately jesting tone of these lines depends partly on *rime riche* links like "cap" and "*cap*italist," "lark" and "*Lark*in," "Hall" and "*hall*mark," and "sky*scrape*r" and "scrape."

But when the poem shifts into a more serious key, the *rime riche* tends to work against it:

> Labour is not accustomed
> To higher living. Railing
> Is gone that I leaned against
> To watch that figure, tall and lean,
> Jim Larkin, shouting, railing.
> Why should he give a damn
> That day for English grammer,
> Arm-waving, eloquent?
>
> (*CP*, 429)

Here the perfect rhyme, with its inevitable hint of light irony, undermines the attempt to create a sympathetic portrait of Larkin. It also distances the reader from Larkin by calling attention to the artificiality of the poem. These lines might be compared with the opening of "Inscription for a Headstone"—"What Larkin bawled to hungry crowds / Is murmured now in dining-hall"—which firmly establishes Larkin's authority, and in which the assonantal link between "bawled" and "dining-hall" works expressively to underscore the contrast between Larkin's times and the present.

The damaging effects of this technique are even more pronounced in the four closing lines of "New Liberty Hall":

> On top, a green pagoda
> Has glorified cement,
> Umbrella'd the sun. Go, da,
> And shiver in your tenement.
>
> (*CP*, 429)

The mocking tone implicit in the connection between "pag*oda*" (an accurate description of the building's roof) and "go, da" undermines the extremely serious point being made here: that labor, turned capitalist, is ignoring the reality confronting those who need its help the most—Ireland's poor. The final line rescues the point somewhat, but the damage has been done, and the overall effect of the passage—and of the poem—falls short of the mark.

The most common objection to Clarke's public poetry has, however, less to do with matters of style or rhetorical stance than the notion that Clarke's work is primarily provincial. Perhaps the best way to respond to this contention is to examine a sequence of three poems that has been praised chiefly as an example of Clarke's abilities as a local satirist. The sequence, published in *Ancient Lights*, is entitled "Three Poems About Children," and has as its immediate subject a fire in a Catholic orphanage in Cavan, near the border with Northern Ireland. The critical attention that this sequence has attracted has focused almost entirely on the third poem, clearly the most satirical.[7] But the poems were meant to be read together, and when they are, they reveal a range that extends considerably beyond the provincial.

Clarke's note to these poems supplies some of the details about the event behind them: "This orphanage was at some distance from the main convent building and the sixty children, trapped in an upper dormitory, without fire escape, were in charge of an elderly lay woman. All perished" (*CP*, 548). A statement made by a local bishop, Clarke adds, inspired the sequence; Clarke's version of that statement appears in the third poem:

> Has not a Bishop declared
> That flame-wrapped babes are spared
> Our life-time of temptation?
>
> (*CP*, 197)

The first poem relies on a contrast between the present and the time of Ireland's Penal Laws in the eighteenth century, when the church was discriminated against and forced to hold its services outside and in secret:

> Better the book against the rock,
> The misery of roofless faith,
> Than all this mockery of time,
> Eternalising of mute souls.
> Though offerings increase, increase,
> The ancient arms can bring no peace,
> When the first breath is unforgiven
> And charity, to find a home,
> Redeems the baby from the breast.
> O, then, at the very font of grace,
> Pity, pity—the dumb must cry.
> Their tiny tears are in the walls
> We build. They turn to dust so soon,
> How can we learn upon our knees,
> That ironside unropes the bell?
>
> (*CP*, 196)

The opening lines argue that the "roofless faith" of the Penal Days is to be preferred to modern Irish Catholicism, which oppresses by devaluing man and his earthly life in favor of eternal salvation—a faith that mocks time by "eternalising mute souls."

The poem's argument is extended beyond the question of the orphanage fire and the bishop's response largely through ambiguity. "When the first breath is unforgiven," for example, refers, on the surface, to the church's views on illegitimate children, and the two following lines attack the practice of taking these children from their mothers and placing them in orphanages like the one in Cavan. But "when the first breath is unforgiven" also refers to the doctrine of original sin, which Clarke sees as lying at the heart of the Catholic Church's anti-humanistic teachings since it sees man as fallen from the moment of birth. On this level, the ironical "redeems" suggests that the church's doctrine of redemption unfairly requires man to choose the spiritual (the loveless "ancient arms" of the church) over the human (the arms and the breast of the mother). Similarly, "their tiny tears are in the walls / We build" again questions the value of orphanages for illegitimate children, but also suggests, more generally, that the walls of the anti-humanistic attitudes that lie behind such institutions can cause human suffering.

This broader notion is furthered in the closing lines. If "ironside" is taken to refer to Cromwell's bigotedly Protestant soldiery, these lines suggest that an unchecked trust in a religious point of view can blind man to cruelty and suffering brought about in the name of religion, specifically the brutal repression by Cromwell of Irish Catholics ("ironside unropes the bell"—the bell, that is, of a church or monastery); and if "ironside" is taken as referring to the inflexible views of Irish Catholicism, the last line suggests that this kind of attitude "unropes the bell" of mourning by depriving the death of the orphans, and of man in general, of any tragic significance. What is being challenged here is not just the bishop's response to the death of the children, but what it represents—a view of man that accepts the "mockery of time" and the "eternalising of mute souls."

The second poem in the sequence, by lamenting the fire as something that has deprived the orphans of human life and love, also argues this point:

> These infants die too quick
> For our salvation, caught up

By a fatal sign from Limbo,
Unfathered in our thought
Before they can share the sky
With us. Though faith allow
Obscurity of being
And clay rejoice: flowers
That wither in the heat
Of benediction, one
By one, are thrown away.
(*CP*, 197)

The phrase "our salvation" implies both that the orphans have been deprived of our life and we of theirs, a reminder that the concept of salvation extends far beyond that of spiritual rescue from the consequences of sin. A similar play on religious language occurs in the poem's final image comparing the burning orphans to flowers "that wither in the heat/Of benediction," an ironic reference to the Catholic devotional service and to the rather easy words of blessing pronounced on the orphans by the bishop. The final line forcefully undermines the bishop's argument that the orphans are fortunate— that their lives are of no inherent value ("faith allow/Obscurity of being"), and that death is to be welcomed as a gateway to eternal salvation ("and clay rejoice"); on the contrary, the poem says, the lives of the children have simply been "thrown away." Moreover, because "thrown away" implies an agent, it points to a suggestion made in the third poem—that the church may bear some responsibility for the deaths.

That the third poem represents Clarke's public poetry at its angriest is not to be denied; the bitterness of this poem must be read, however, in the larger context established in the first two poems. The shift from the philosophical tone of the first two poems to the unmitigated satirical offensive of the third is signaled partly by a change from the unrhymed verse of the first poem and the muted assonance of the second to couplets joined by standard rhyme and variations of standard rhyme:

Martyr and heretic
Have been the shrieking wick!
But smoke of faith on fire
Can hide us from enquiry

And trust in Providence
Rid us of vain expense.
So why should pity uncage
A burning orphanage,
Bar flight to little souls
That set no churchbell tolling?

Cast-iron step and rail
Could but prolong the wailing:
Has not a Bishop declared
That flame-wrapped babes are spared
Our life-time of temptation?
Leap, mind, in consolation
For heart can only lodge
Itself, plucked out by logic.
Those children, charred in Cavan,
Passed straight through Hell to Heaven.

(*CP*, 197)

Part of the poem's rhetorical strategy depends on a direct appeal to the emotions, and the opening lines, especially the image of a "shrieking wick," introduce this immediately. The poem also depends on irony, as in the following four lines, cynically suggesting that the bishop's statement might be a means of covering up negligence on the church's part. (Clarke's note to the poem, referring to the distance from orphanage to convent, the lack of a fire escape, and the possibility of inadequate supervision, also points to this possibility.) The final couplet depends both on emotional appeal and irony. The irony is enhanced by the feminine half-rhyme. The emotional appeal also depends on the pairing of "Cavan" and "heaven," particularly in the final impression that it leaves of a very real and painful hell versus a remote and now somewhat discredited heaven.

Despite its rather narrow satirical intention, this poem raises broader questions that connect it to the first two poems of the sequence. The lines hinting at a possible covering up of church negligence also suggest that theories of consolation such as that offered by the bishop represent attempts to avoid any meaningful philosophical "enquiry" into the tragic events of this world and the "expense" of trying to come to terms with such events without the crutch of religion (the "smoke of faith") that explains human suffering as part of God's mysterious providence.[8] Also, the poem opposes the spirit of religious consolation with the very human values of pity and love.

"Three Poems About Children" offers considerably more than a scathing response to the statement of an insensitive Irish cleric. It challenges the philosophy that lies behind that statement, and argues for the worth of human experience and human dignity. As such, it stands as an impressive example of how Clarke, in the best of his public poetry, was able to meet what he saw as the modern Irish poet's responsibility to comment on social and political reality, while, at the same time, fulfilling the more far-reaching role of a poet concerned with the human condition.

6

"The World's Mad Business" (II): Longer Public Poems

Flight to Africa includes a relatively long poem entitled "Cypress Grove" that, in its conclusion, attacks the spread of suburbia that engulfed the neighborhood of Clarke's home in Templeogue:

> The sewered city with a rump of suburbs
> Has reached the pillared gate in its expansion,
> Design of the daffodils, the urns, disturbed by
> Air-scrooging builders, men who buy and sell fast.
> One Gallagher bought the estate. Now concrete-mixers
> Vomit new villas: builder, they say, from Belfast
> With his surveyors turning down the oil-wicks.
> The shadow is going out from Cypress Grove,
> The solemn branches echoing our groan,
> Where open carriages, barouches, drove:
> Walnut, rare corktree, torn up by machine.
> I hear the shrills of the electric saw
> Lopping the shelter, unsapping the winter-green
> For wood-yards, miss at breakfast time the cawing
> Of local rooks. Many have moved to Fortrose.
> They hear in my lifted hand a gun-report,
> Scatter their peace in another volley.
>   I stare:
> Elegant past blown out like a torchère.
>
>   (*CP*, 286)

The tone of the first seven lines in this passage is the familiar one of

Clarke the satirist lashing out at conditions that he sees as detrimental to modern Ireland. But the rest of the passage is markedly different; it is much more personal than poems such as "Celebrations" and "Mother and Child," and bears the signs more of a private lament than of a piece of social satire.

This combination of strident invective and reflective subjectivity is characteristic of several relatively long public poems that Clarke wrote in the 1950s and 1960s.[1] In these poems, the satire is usually directed at the materialistic attitudes evident in the "air-scrooging builders" of "Cypress Grove," while the subjectivity often provides a way of arguing for humanistic values that Clarke sees as threatened by modern materialism. These poems also rely on Clarke's personal voice and on his experience as a poet to explore the responsibility of the artist in a society that ignores art and the values that it stands for.

"The Loss of Strength" (*Too Great a Vine*) is a prominent example of this mode. It conflates public and private by drawing a parallel between Clarke's life and Ireland. Both, as the title of the poem suggests, are at an ebb. Clarke was sixty-one when the poem was published, and he had just recovered from a serious illness;[2] moreover, his reputation was declining, as evidenced by the publication of *Too Great A Vine* in a small private edition. And Ireland, in Clarke's view, was suffering from the illness of rampant materialism and the social and political domination of a conservative and inhibiting Catholic Church.

The poem opens with a description of the destruction of nature by the steady advance of materialistic "progress":

> Farm-brooks that come down to Rathfarnham
> By grange-wall, tree-stop, from the hills,
> Might never have heard the rustle in barn dance,
> The sluicing, bolting, of their flour-mills,
> Nor have been of use in the steady reel
> On step-boards of the iron wheel-rim,
> For Dublin crowds them in: they wheeze now
> Beneath new pavements, name old laneways,
> Discharge, excrete, their centuries,
> Man-trapped in concrete, deeper drainage.
> Yet, littling by itself, I found one
> That had never run to town.
>
> (*CP*, 212)

Nature's loss of strength, paralleling Clarke's and Ireland's, is expressed here in the image of the farm-brooks poisoned by the city. The stanza also suggests that this loss is a symptom of a deeper deprivation, the destruction of a way of life in which men lived in harmony with nature, harnessing its power rather than destroying it. Moreover, the reference to "the rustle in barn dance" implies that this way of life also included harmony between human beings and an uninhibited enjoyment of life's pleasures.

The path to recovering that life and those values is hinted at in the third stanza, which describes, with moving conviction, Clarke's loss of physical strength:

> I climb among the hills no more
> To taste a last water, hide in cloud-mist
> From sheep and goat. The days are downpour.
> Cycle is gone, warm patch on trousers.
> All, all, drive faster, stink without,
> Spirit and spark within, no doubt.
> When hope was active, I stood taller
> Than my own sons. Beloved strength
> Springs past me, three to one. Halldoor
> Keeps open, estimates the length
> To which I go: a mile to tire-a.
> But I knew the stone beds of Ireland.
>
> (CP, 212)

The "stone beds of Ireland" are more than a memory. They are, first, the source of the farm-brooks of stanza one, and so represent the importance of nature that is ignored by modern materialism. They also suggest the bedrock of Irish culture, the source of Irish art. As the end of the poem makes clear, it is to this source that Clarke as a poet and Ireland as a nation must remain true if they are to recover their strength. In the juxtaposition of Clarke's nostalgic memories ("Cycle is gone, warm patch on trousers") with an ironic observation on modern, motorized society ("All, all, drive faster, stink without/Spirit and spark within, no doubt"), this stanza also demonstrates Clarke's ability to conflate private and public.

In a flashback that follows this stanza, Clarke recalls in more detail his youthful explorations of the Irish countryside and his enthusiasm for the pagan legends that inspired his early poetry:

Beclipped and confident of shank,
I rode the plain with chain that freed me.
On a rim akin to air, I cranked up
Standstill of gradient, freewheeled
Down glens beyond our national school,
Our catechism and British rule,
To find, thought I, the very roc's nest
A-spar on Diamond Hill; clouted
By wind, strawing the narrowest sea-lough,
A speck that saw a cloud put out
A goose-neck, counting far below
The Twelve Pins in a row.

The young must have a solitude
To feel the strength in mind, restore
Small world of liking. Saints have spewed
Too much. I wanted test of stories
Our poets had talked about, pinmeal
To potboil long ago. Cloud-feelers
Featherers, touched our restlessness.
Lost prosody restrained us. Summit
Showed valleys, reafforesting,
The Fianna, leaf-veined, among them.
Now only a wishing-cap could leave me
On the top of Slieve Mish.

(*CP*, 213)

Here the natural beauty of rural Ireland, and the pagan legends that Clarke tracked through it, represent a freedom from the constraints that Clarke found around him as an Irish Catholic growing up in Dublin—constraints that have become, Clarke would insist, dominant in modern Ireland.

The two-line lament that concludes this memory brings the poem back to the present, and in the following stanza, Clarke questions not just the visible signs of the Ireland that has tried to destroy these routes to freedom, but also the attitudes that lie behind them:

Shannoning from the tide, a sea-god
Became our servant once, demeaned
Himself, a three-legged, slippery body:
Uncatchable, being submarine,

He spoked the hub. Now engineering
Machinery destroys the weirs,
Directs, monk-like, our natural flow:
Yet it was pleasant at Castleconnell
To watch the salmon brighten their raincoats.
The reeds wade out for what is gone:
That mile of spray faraway on the rapids
Is hidden in a tap.

                              (*CP*, 213)

In the reference to "engineering / Machinery," Clarke is not objecting
to the Shannon hydroelectric plant *per se*, but to the materialistic
outlook that makes decisions about building such facilities only on
grounds of profit and loss, ignoring the human costs of such develop-
ments. Just as the concrete that "man-trapped" the farm-brooks in
stanza one represents a loss more fundamental than the damage done
to the streams themselves, so the hydroelectric plant is seen here as a
force working not merely against the natural world, but also, particu-
larly because of the connection made between the Shannon and
pre-Christian Ireland, against a way of life in which men respected
nature and lived in harmony with it. The phrase "monk-like" also calls
to mind the tension in *Pilgrimage* between religious asceticism and
sexual freedom. Modern materialism, represented by the hydroelec-
tric plant, ignores human values and pleasures, including the sexual
pleasures alluded to in "our natural flow," just as the medieval monks
ignored those qualities—and just as the Catholic Church, in Clarke's
view, ignores them in modern Ireland.

        This argument is spelled out two stanzas later in a passage that
recalls Clarke's discovery of the world of medieval monasticism:

Thousands ply the wonted scissors,
Cut up the immaterial, take
Our measure. When the soul is body-busy,
Rhyme interferes for its own sake
But gets no credit. Late in the day,
Then, coasting back from Milltown Malbay,
I saw before bell rang a warning,
Scattery Island and its round tower.

A child was scorching by that corner
To hurl me back, unknottable power,
Hell-fire in twist and turn, grotesque:
Now, Celtic-Romanesque.

(*CP*, 214)

One of the great evils of modern life, in Clarke's view, is the willing-
ness to ignore "the immaterial," to think that it is possible to take the
measure of everything and reduce it to quantifiable data that can be
analyzed in terms of profit and loss. For Clarke, such thinking leads
just as inevitably to the betrayal of intangible values like human love
and freedom as do the puritanical strictures of modern Irish Catholi-
cism. The recollection of Clarke's interest in medieval Ireland raises
the question of the function of art in a society dominated by materi-
alism and anti-humanistic religious teachings. In the new Ireland, a
society in which "the soul is body-busy," art is seen as immaterial and
therefore irrelevant. And so "Rhyme interferes for its sake / But gets
no credit"—an accurate description of Clarke's status as a poet when
"The Loss of Strength" was written.

Before trying to resolve the question of what the poet's role
should be in a society that has no place for art, "The Loss of Strength"
examines a later phase of Irish history, the period of the Norman
invasion in the twelfth century. Clarke sees in this age an overthrow-
ing and corrupting of the "stone beds of Ireland":

Too great a vine, they say, can sour
The best of clay. No pair of sinners
But learned saints had overpowered
Our country, Malachi the Thin
And Bernard of Clairvaux. Prodigious
In zeal, these cooled and burned our porridge.
(Later came breakspear, strong bow backing)
The arch sprang wide for their Cistercians.
O bread was wersh and well was brack.
War rattled at us in hammered shirts:
An Englishman had been the Pontiff.
They marched to Mellifont.

(*CP*, 216)

Clarke is concerned here not only with the military invasion of Ireland by Strongbow and his Norman forces, but also with the arrival of Continental orders of monasticism (the Cistercians), headed by their chief architect, Bernard of Clairvaux, and later by his pupil Malachi, who founded Mellifont Abbey in 1142. As the Norman invasion represented an attempt to overthrow Ireland's native Gaelic tradition, so the arrival of Bernard and his followers represented, in Clarke's view, a corruption of Ireland's native religious tradition and an unfortunate heightening of its ascetic tendencies. Moreover, as was argued in the stanza on the Shannon hydroelectric plant, there is a connection between the religious zeal of monks like Bernard and Malachi and the materialistic ambitions of modern developers. Both, as the next stanza suggests, destroy the Irish past and its values:

> But time goes back. Monks, whom we praise now,
> Take down a castle, stone by stone,
> To make an abbey, restore the chain-light
> Of silence. Gelignite has blown up
> Too much: yet on the Hill of Allen,
> The blasters are at work. Gallon
> By gallon our roads go. Stonecrushers
> Must feed them. Fionn hunted here, Oisín
> Complained of age. I think of rushed bones,
> Bogland, in furnaces, grown greener,
> The prophecy of Colmcille—
> Car without horse—fulfilled.
>
> (*CP*, 216)

The poem closes by returning to the problem of the poet's role in a society dominated by such forces:

> Loss but repeats the startling legend
> Of time. A poet wants no more
> To palliate his mind, edging
> Worn cards behind a shaky door
> Or tinting them until the puce
> Shuffle the purple. May the Deuce
> Take all of them and thought get better
> While faith and country play a far hand!

Plod on, tired rhyme. The streams that wetted
Forgotten wheels push past Rathfarnham,
Half underground: slime steps on stone.
I count them—not my own.

(CP, 217)

These lines can be read as a statement about Clarke's turning to public poetry and abandoning the "worn cards" of his earlier religious lyrics. But the stanza also recognizes that public poetry, to be of any value, must go beyond specific satirical attacks; it must also express the importance of human values and feelings, must tap the strength of a past world in which those qualities were honored, not neglected and circumscribed. In its closing image, the poem returns to its beginning, the "farm-brooks that come down to Rathfarnham"; the secret lies there, in the world that these streams represent—the world of nature, but also that of Irish tradition, the "stone beds of Ireland." If that world is buried, "half underground" or "man-trapped in concrete," the poet must find a way to dig it up, because it, and the values that it stands for, are the modern Irish poet's true subject and his means of recovering his—and his country's—strength.

Clarke attempts precisely that unearthing of human values in perhaps the most impressive of his longer public poems, "Forget Me Not" (1962). And this poem makes that attempt in the context of a far more local target for its satire than unplanned suburban growth: the slaughtering of Irish horses for export to Europe as meat. Clarke became particularly incensed about this practice when forty-eight horses that had been shipped to the Continent for slaughter were lost in a storm at sea; in response, protection societies in Ireland advocated not an end to horse slaughtering but rather the establishment of abattoirs in Ireland. To read "Forget Me Not," however, as chiefly a protest against this practice, as at least one critic has done,[3] is to miss the point of the poem, to see only the symptom under attack and not the more important human issues lying beneath it. In Clarke's view the practice of slaughtering horses for profit is closely related to the building of facilities such as the hydroelectric plant at Shannon and to the spread of suburban developments; all these actions reflect a materialistic philosophy that ignores values such as love and freedom. In "Forget Me Not," Clarke uses the horse trade as a way of attacking what Donald Davie has called the "sacrilege" of neglecting the special, centuries-old relationship between horse and man,[4] and, more important, of neglecting the humanistic principles that should govern the relationship between man and man.

"Forget Me Not" also recognizes that the poet has an important role to play in maintaining those principles, in rescuing humanistic values from the extinction with which they are threatened by modern materialism. The poem opens by calling attention to the relationship between art and reality:

> *Up the hill,*
> *Hurry me not;*
> *Down the hill,*
> *Worry me not;*
> *On the level,*
> *Spare me not,*
> *In the stable,*
> *Forget me not.*

> Trochaic dimeter, amphimacer
> And choriamb, with hyper catalexis,
> Grammatical inversion, springing of double
> Rhyme. So we learned to scan all, analyse
> Lyric and ode, elegy, anonymous patter,
> For what is song itself but substitution?
>   (*CP*, 237)

Davie has shown how these lines, with their accurate prosodic description of the song recalled from Clarke's childhood, suggest that the passing of the horse from everyday life may well have altered the rhythms of poetry.[5] And the deliberately uneven rhythms and irregular verse paragraphs of "Forget Me Not" make the point that *this* is a poem written without benefit of the regular rhythms of another age. But more than poetry has been altered since the days of the horse. As Davie also points out, the pun in "substitution" argues for an extremely close connection between art and reality,[6] and "Forget Me Not" is chiefly concerned with the changes in the world of reality that have taken place since the disappearance of the horse. In a passage following the one quoted above, Clarke spells out the values that he sees as threatened by modern civilization:

> Coleridge had picked
> That phrase for us—*vergiss-mein-nicht*, emblem
> Of love and friendship, delicate sentiments.
> (*CP*, 237)

These are the humanistic qualities—"love and friendship, delicate sentiments"—that the poem is arguing for and opposing to the values of a society that unthinkingly slaughters horses for profit.

To convey those qualities, "Forget Me Not" relies chiefly on Clarke's boyhood memories of a world in which the horse was the object of man's respect and affection.[7] The verse-paragraph following the one on Coleridge shifts the poem into this subjective mode:

> Child climbed
> Into the trap; the pony started quick
> As fly to a flick and Uncle John began
> Our work-a-day, holiday jingle.
> (*CP*, 237)

The internal rhyme in the last line underscores the point that this was a time when work and pleasure went hand in hand, and when the horse was important to both. It also suggests a harmony between man and the natural world similar to that expressed in the image of "the sluicing, bolting, of their flour-mills" in "The Loss of Strength."

The affection between man and horse hinted at in this passage is expressed more forcefully in another childhood memory:

> Horse-heads above me,
> Below me. Happy on tram top, I looked down
> On plaited manes, alighted safely, caught
> Sidelong near kerb, perhaps, affectionate glance
> As I passed a blinker. Much to offend the pure:
> Let-down or drench, the sparrows pecking at fume,
> The scavengers with shovel, broom. But, O
> When horse fell down, pity was there: we saw
> Such helplessness, girth buckled, no knack in knee,
> Half-upturned legs—big hands that couldn't unclench.
> (*CP*, 239)

This passage shows how Clarke manages to express with conviction, and without lapsing into sentimentality, feelings like affection and pity. The wealth of concrete detail accounts in part for this, especially the conspicuously specific description of the horse relieving itself. Coming between the affectionate glance of the horse and the pity felt by the man, it firmly anchors the scene in reality, rescuing it from any tendency to drift toward sentimental idealism. Most of the passages in "Forget Me Not" dealing with Clarke's childhood memories work this way; by vividly recreating the world of Clarke's youth, a world in which horses and men lived and worked in harmony, they express the experience of love and friendship that lies at the heart of the poem.

The satirical passages occur only after this context of feeling has been established, and when the attack on the horse trade comes, it is aimed chiefly at the violation of humanistic values. The transition to the satirical mode demonstrates Clarke's mastery of the flexible form used in "Forget Me Not":

> . . . Let joy cast off a trace, for once,
> High-stepping beyond the Phoenix Monument
> In the long ago of British rule, I saw
> With my own eyes a white horse that unfabled
> The Unicorn.
>
> Mechanized vehicles:
> Horse-power by handle-turn. My Uncle John
> Lost stable companions, drivers, all. Though poor,
> He kept his last mare out on grass. They aged
> Together. At twenty-one, I thought it right
> And proper.
>
> How could I know that greed
> Spreads quicker than political hate? No need
> Of propaganda. Good company, up and down
> The ages, gone: the trick of knife left, horse cut
> To serve man. All the gentling, custom of mind
> And instinct, close affection, done with. The unemployed
> Must go. Dead or ghosted by froths, we ship them
> Abroad. Foal, filly, farm pony, bred for slaughter:
> What are they now but hundredweights of meat?
>
> (CP, 240)

The abrupt shift from Clarke's memory of the white horse to "Mechanized vehicles" jolts the poem from the past into the unhappy present. The verse-paragraph on the sacrifices that Clarke's Uncle John made for his last mare sets up by means of contrast the charge made in the next verse-paragraph about the greed that motivates the horse trade. The emphasis in this attack falls on the loss of qualities such as "Good company," "gentling custom of mind," "instinct," and "close affection" brought about by a society that accepts the slaughtering of horses.

As in "The Loss of Strength," the last voice heard in "Forget Me Not" is that of the poet searching for a way to keep his art alive in a materialistic world that has no use for it or the values that it expresses:

> . . . Tipsters respect our grand sires,
> Thorough-breds, jumpers o' the best.
> Our grass still makes a noble show, and the roar
> Of money cheers us at the winning post.
> So pack tradition in the meat-sack, Boys,
> Write off the epitaph of Yeats.
> I'll turn
> To jogtrot, pony bell, say my first lesson:

> *Up the hill,*
> *Hurry me not;*
> *Down the hill,*
> *Worry me not;*
> *On the level,*
> *Spare me not,*
> *In the stable,*
> *Forget me not.*

> *Forget me not.*

(*CP*, 242–243)

Confronted with a world that appreciates horses only to the extent that they can make a profit, either in the abbatoir or at the racetrack, Clarke turns to the past: the "slime steps on stone" in "The Loss of Strength," "jogtrot, pony bell . . . my first lesson" in this poem. In the final line, which repeats the last line of the horse's song, the poet's voice is heard over that of the horse; in his plea of *"Forget me not,"* the poet is asking that he and his art, and the humanistic values that he is speaking for, not be forgotten. This is the appeal that lies behind Clarke's public poetry as a whole, and that makes it, at its best, not merely the expression of an outraged twentieth-century Irishman, but rather of a human being concerned about other human beings.

A final clue to the humanistic vision behind Clarke's public poetry can be found in his attitude toward the one Irish writer who, more than any other, stood as a model to an Irishman setting out to write satire: Jonathan Swift. Clarke found much to admire in Swift, including the frequently glossed-over scatological side of his work. Swift's emphasis on physicality, especially as a way of revealing the gap between the ideal and the real, is reflected in Clarke's "Martha Blake at Fifty One" (*Flight to Africa*), a sequel to "Martha Blake" of *Night and Morning*. The protagonist of the later poem is an extremely devout Catholic, disdaining the physical side of life, and Clarke, with all the ruthless realism of Swift, argues that such an attitude is self-deceiving:

> She suffered from dropped stomach, heartburn
>> Scalding, water-brash
> And when she brought her wind up, turning
>> Red with the weight of mashed
> Potato, mint could not relieve her.
>> In vain her many belches,
> For all below was swelling, heaving
>> Wamble, gurgle, squealch.
>
> She lay on the sofa with her legs up,
>> A decade on her lip,
> At four o'clock, taking a cup
>> Of lukewarm water, sip
> By sip, but still her daily food
>> Repeated and the bile
> Tormented her. In a blue hood,
>> The Virgin sadly smiled.
>
>   (*CP*, 266)

Clarke also admired Swift's powers as a satirist. Swift's influence on Clarke's satirical style can be seen in "Knacker Rhymes (I)" (*The Horse-Eaters*), a poem, like "Forget Me Not," prompted by the decision to build abattoirs in Ireland:

Don't ship, kill, can them
First—abattoirs pay—
Or chill the carcases
For hook and tray;
Packed, sacked, quay-stacked,
The neighless all saved
From wavetops, ill-treatment
Abroad. Our meat-trade
Respected: thousands
Bred yearly will fatten
Small farmers, browse,
Idle as cattle.
But why keep the raw hides
And none of the insides?
Let stomach be steady, then,
As hand that endorses
The bigger cheques. Irishmen,
Taste your own horses!
                    (*CP*, 222)

As in Swift's A *Modest Proposal*, the ironic mask is never dropped in this poem, and the final suggestion that Irishmen eat their own horses is made with the same apparent sincerity as the suggestion in Swift's work that Irishmen eat their own children.[8]

But whatever the importance to Clarke of Swift's scatological verse or his satirical writings, ultimately the connection between these two men is more far-reaching. To see this, one must turn to "A Sermon on Swift" (*A Sermon on Swift and Other Poems*, 1968), which describes Clarke's experience giving a talk on Swift in St. Patrick's Cathedral as part of the Swift tercentenary celebrations in 1967. In this poem, Clarke expresses admiration for Swift's satirical powers, and suggests that the Swift who created "Celia on a close-stool" and "Corrina, / Taking herself to pieces at midnight" influenced his own work: "Swift wrote of privy matters / That have to be my text" (both in the sense of the text of his tercentenary speech and of his poetry in general).

But Swift's most profound significance for Clarke is expressed in the passage that ends the poem:

. . . My hour, above
Myself, draws to an end. Satiric rhymes
Are safe in the Deanery. So, I must find
A moral, search among my wits.

I have

It.

In his sudden poem *The Day of Judgment*
Swift borrowed the allegoric bolt of Jove,
Damned and forgave the human race, dismissed
The jest of life. Here is his secret belief
For sure: the doctrine of Erigena,
Scribing his way from West to East, from bang
Of monastery door, click o' the latch,
His sandals worn out, unsoled, a voice proclaiming
The World's mad business—Eternal Absolution.

(*CP*, 460)

In Clarke's view, however much Swift appeared to damn the human race in his satire, he also was capable of forgiving it.[9] For Clarke, in other words, Swift wrote not out of hatred or bitterness, but out of an underlying faith in mankind. The link that Clarke draws between Swift and Erigena, the ninth-century Irish philosopher and theologian, makes this even more clear; like Swift (and like Clarke), Erigena believed in the power of human reason, but he also believed that all men were an integral part of a divine process and so were fundamentally good, not evil. Here lies the "secret belief" behind Clarke's public poetry, the same belief that was found in the poems of *Pilgrimage* and *Night and Morning*: a humanistic faith in man's essential goodness and in his capacity for improving his own life and the lives of others. At his best, Clarke the public poet can be seen precisely as Clarke saw Swift—as a kind of contemporary Erigena, "scribing his way" through the problems and shortcomings of his native country, often ignored, occasionally damned, frequently disillusioned, but never losing his faith in humankind, always, one way or another, "proclaiming / The World's mad business—Eternal Absolution."

7
"The Oracle, Not Yet Dumb" (I):
Mnemosyne Lay in Dust

In 1962, one year after the publication of *Later Poems* had put him on the literary map,[1] Clarke visited Greece, where he saw Mount Parnassus, the ancient symbol of poetic inspiration; he recorded the experience in a poem entitled "Mount Parnassus," published in *Flight to Africa*:

> Never have I been in the south
> So far from self and yet I must
> Learn, straight from the horse's mouth,
> To kick up my own dust.
> Here is the source. Here was our must.
> I see no flowers to grass us,
> Only the scale of Mount Parnassus:
> Simplicity of snow
> Above, the pillared drouth,
> The worn-out, below.
> I stray from American, German, tourists,
> Greek guide, feel in my two wrists
> Answer for which I have come,
> The Oracle, not yet dumb.
>
> (*CP*, 245)

The Oracle was indeed not yet dumb for Clarke. In fact, with the publication of *Flight to Africa* in 1963, Clarke began, at the age of sixty-seven, the most prolific phase of his career; in the last twelve years of his life, he published a greater volume and a far greater variety of poetry than in all the years before. The books that appeared in an astonishingly steady flow in these years—*Flight to Africa* (1963), *Mnemosyne Lay in Dust* (1966), *Old-Fashioned Pilgrimage* (1967), *The Echo at Coole* (1968), *A Sermon on Swift* (1968), *Orphide* (1970), and *Tiresias* (1971)—included, in addition to the satirical verse discussed in the two previous chapters, personal poems relying on a confessional mode, descriptive and travel poems, poems about other Irish literary figures, free translations of poems from the Irish, and erotic poems, including several narratives based on Irish and classical legend.

Despite some flaws—poems that are merely coarse or trivial (from "Impotence": "Enwrinkled as the fig-leaf of Cupid, / Booby can do no more than piddle"), and poems that indulge inappropriately in technical tricks (from "Old-Fashioned Pilgrimage": "He paid for the bluff chiselling: Walt Whitman / Awaiting the Resurrection. Why should you care a whit, man?")—these books contain much to admire. And admire them many readers, Irish and non-Irish, did. The appearance of *Later Poems* in England and America under the imprint of Oxford University Press had brought Clarke to the attention of many non-Irish readers for the first time, and *Flight to Africa* and the volumes that followed it—also distributed in England and America—continued to spread Clarke's reputation. All his books published in the 1960s and 1970s received generous recognition in the British and American press, and many reviewers shared Denis Donoghue's judgment that Clarke was "an artist who was tardy in recognizing where his strength lay."[2]

For all the long-deserved acclaim that statements such as Donoghue's gave Clarke, they also did him some disservice. The sudden flurry of critical attention that Clarke won in his last twelve years focused chiefly on the poems that were coming out at the time, and so tended to neglect the earlier work, especially *Pilgrimage* and *Night and Morning*. This neglect often meant that those who praised Clarke's poetry of the 1960s and 1970s failed to see that, for all its variety, it grows out of the same struggle with religious prohibition documented in *Pilgrimage* and *Night and Morning*, and has at its center the same humanistic vision that informs Clarke's work from beginning to end.

The best of Clarke's later poems, excluding the public poems, can be grouped into three categories, each of which will be treated in a separate chapter: (1) personal poems, *Mnemosyne Lay in Dust* being the most significant, which owe much to the confessional mode of *Night and Morning*; (2) erotic poems; and (3) free translations of Gaelic poems, reflecting Clarke's lifelong commitment to the Gaelic tradition.

One of the lessons that Clarke describes himself as seeking to learn from the Mount Parnassus Oracle is how "to kick up my own dust," and a number of Clarke's later poems, polar opposites to most of the public poetry of the same period, take this lesson to heart. The most significant of these introspective and confessional poems is *Mnemosyne Lay in Dust* (1966), a long and highly acclaimed poem dealing with Clarke's mental breakdown as a young man and the thirteen months that he spent in St. Patrick's Hospital, a mental institution in Dublin.[3] A passage in *Twice Round the Black Church* provides a context for *Mnemosyne Lay in Dust* and describes some of the experiences of his mental breakdown:

> But in the years of adolescent mental struggle, I had felt motherless and carried my resentment into the next world, so that to this day I dislike the hyperdulia which is increasing in town and country. I did not realize how deeply I felt that growing loss until I was in my twenties and was dangerously ill in body and mind. For months I existed in a visional state which was heightened by the usual opiates. In a continual dream-sequence I followed the exploits of a Republican fighter in Limerick and the southern counties and at times his breathless escapes seemed mine. Other visions were eastern and I can remember countless Jewish children hurrying at nightfall through an immense gateway into a garden, so exquisite was the olive-and-ivory of their faces. One day I awoke in hot summer sunshine and, looking down the ward, noticed that the head of the patient in the last bed, on the right, was on the pillow beside him. I watched for a long time that strange sight, believing that I was suffering from an illusion, but the head with its closed eyes and short beard remained several inches away from the man's body. In my confused state of mind, I felt sure that he was St. John the Baptist.[4]

These visions, and several others, are recounted in *Mnemosyne Lay in Dust*. Indeed, one of the poem's major achievements is the realistic force with which it describes the horrors of mental illness.

But the poem's significance extends considerably beyond this. The breakdown of Maurice Devane (the poem's protagonist) is brought about by an overwhelming burden of guilt and self-degradation, feelings that Clarke associated, especially in his earlier poetry, with his Irish Catholic upbringing and its view of men as inherently sinful. In its portrayal of Maurice's illness, *Mnemosyne Lay in Dust* documents with great conviction the damaging effects of that vision of man, and in its recounting of Maurice's recovery, asserts with equal conviction Clarke's humanistic faith in man's dignity and freedom.

The poem opens in the darkness of Dublin at dusk, but also in the inner gloom of a man for whom life and its pleasures are "beyond himself":

> Past the house where he was got
> In darkness, terrace, provision shop,
> Wing-hidden convent opposite,
> Past public-houses at lighting-up
> Time, crowds outside them—Maurice Devane
> Watched from the taxi window in vain
> National stir and gaiety
> Beyond himself: St. Patrick's Day,
> The spike-ends of the Blue Coat school,
> Georgian houses, ribald gloom
> Rag-shadowed by gaslight, quiet pavements
> > Moon-waiting in Blackhall Place.
> >   (*CP*, 327)

The deliberately uneven rhythms and awkward runovers in this stanza help convey the uncertainty and dissociation that Maurice experiences in his disturbed state. The darkness of Maurice's vision is expressed partly through sound patterns, especially the echoes between "blue," "school," "gloom," and "*moon*-waiting," and partly through images, particularly "the spike-ends of the Blue Coat school," suggesting the oppressive nature of Maurice's own schooling.

The stanza does more, however, than mirror Maurice's confusion and oppression. The runover between the first two lines, in addition to the rhythmic disturbance that it creates, underscores the word "got," and so calls attention to the brutality of the phrase "where he was got." The runover also emphasizes that this act of conception took place "in darkness," the darkness of a point of view that uses degrading language such as "where he was got" to talk about the act of love. This view of human sexuality—a view that Clarke ascribes to the Irish Catholic Church—appears again in one of Maurice's hallucinatory visions later in the poem:

> The shriek of women with upswollen
> Bodies, held down in torment, rolling
> And giving birth to foundlings, shriek
> After shriek, the blanket lifting unspeakable
> Protrusions. . . .
>
> (*CP*, 329)

Here the act of birth is seen as a nightmare of repulsive suffering, part of the "ribald gloom" that Maurice must free himself from if he is to recover his sanity.

In *A Penny in the Clouds*, Clarke attributes his mental breakdown partly to the conflict between his natural instincts and his strict religious upbringing. "Unfortunately," he says, "neither the pins-and-needles of the galvanic battery nor the black puddings saved me from collapse in a few months, because there is no cure for the folly of youth or the dire consequence of overindulgence in continence."[5] Maurice's collapse has the same cause, as the second stanza of *Mnemosyne Lay in Dust* indicates:

> For six weeks Maurice had not slept,
> Hours pillowed him from right to left side,
> Unconsciousness became the pit
> Of terror. Void would draw his spirit,
> Unself him. Sometimes he fancied that music,
> Soft lights in Surrey, Kent, could cure him,
> Hypnotic touch, until, one evening,
> The death-chill seemed to mount from feet
> To shin, to thigh. Life burning in groin
> And prostate ached for a distant joy.
> But nerves need solitary confinement.
>   Terror repeals the mind.
>
> (*CP*, 327)

Natural impulses and feelings ("life burning in groin") can be repressed only at great cost, the destruction, ultimately, of man's faith in himself and his reason ("terror repeals the mind").

The effect of that destruction is portrayed dramatically in the

sixth section of the poem. The opening stanza finds Maurice confront-
ing darkness, literal and figurative:

> One night he heard heart-breaking sound.
> It was a sigh unworlding its sorrow.
> Another followed. Slowly he counted
> Four different sighs, one after another.
> 'My mother,' he anguished, 'and my sisters
> Have passed away. I am alone, now,
> Lost in myself in a mysterious
> Darkness, the victim in a story.'
> Far whistle of a train, the voice of steam.
> Evil was peering through the peep-hole.
>   (CP, 335)

These thoughts of death (recalling "the death chill" of the first section)
and of being lost and alone lead to a violent breakdown, and in the
next stanza, which describes that breakdown, the relatively quiet and
reflective tone of the first stanza gives way to panic:

> Suddenly heart began to beat
> Too quickly, too loudly. It clamoured
> As if it were stopping. He left the heat
> And stumbled forward, hammered
> The door, called out that he was dying.
> Key turned. Body was picked up, carried
> Beyond the ward, the bedwhite row
> Of faces, into a private darkness.
> Lock turned. He cried out. All was still.
> He stood, limbs shivering in the chill.
>   (CP, 335)

The trochaic inversion in "Suddenly" signals the shift in tone. The
muted assonance of the first stanza is replaced by strong rhymes, and
syntactical and line units, unlike those in the first stanza, are often at
odds, reflecting Maurice's terror. The nervous, staccato movement of
extremely short sentences further underscores Maurice's panic, and
the use of distinctly impersonal phrases and constructions reflects his
loss of identity.[6]

The chief symptom of Maurice's illness is loss of memory, but in
the "private darkness" of a padded cell, his memory is suddenly
triggered. What he recalls, however, is an instance of the "dire

consequences of overindulgence in continence," an unhappy love affair with a girl named Margaret (the name that Clarke uses in *Twice Round the Black Church* to refer to his first wife[7]):

> The key had turned again. Blankets
> Were flung into blackness as if to mock
> The cringer on the floor. He wrapped
> The bedclothes around his limbs, shocked back
> To sanity. Lo! in memory yet,
> Margaret came in a frail night-dress,
> Feet bare, her heavy plaits let down
> Between her knees, his pale protectress.
> Nightly restraint, unwanted semen
> Had ended their romantic dream.
>
> (*CP*, 335–336)

Although the "nightly restraint" of fear and guilt destroyed the relationship, this erotic memory is valuable as a sign that Maurice may find a way out of his darkness; he is, temporarily anyway, "shocked back / To sanity."

However, the negative implications of this recollection soon win out over its erotic suggestiveness, and in the next stanza, the last in section six, Maurice sinks to the nadir of his illness, losing control even of his bodily functions:

> Early next morning, he awakened,
> Saw only greyness shining down
> From a skylight on the grey walls
> Of leather, knew, in anguish, his bowels
> Had opened. He turned, shivering, all shent.
> Wrapping himself in the filthied blankets,
> Fearful of dire punishment,
> He waited there until a blankness
> Enveloped him. . . When he raised his head up,
> Noon-light was gentle in the bedroom.
>
> (*CP*, 336)

The description of Maurice as wrapped in "the filthied blankets" of guilt and "fearful of dire punishment" parallels the vision of Clarke himself and of his various personae in *Pilgrimage* and *Night and Morning*.

The "gentle" light that Maurice discovers at the end of the stanza suggests that he may find a way out of the darkness of religious prohibition. That he still has the power to do so is evident in the stanza that opens the next section of the poem:

> Beyond the rack of thought, he passed
> From sleep to sleep. He was unbroken
> Yet. Religion could not cast
> Its multitudinous torn cloak
> About him. Somewhere there was peace
> That drew him towards the nothingness
> Of all. He gave up, tried to cease
> Himself, but delicately clinging
> To this and that, life drew him back
> To drip of water-torment, rack.
>
> (*CP*, 336)

The stanza breaks into two related statements. In the first, Maurice is "unbroken," still capable of living without the false comfort of religion's "torn cloak." This religion, like the sleep that Maurice is drifting through, is attractive because it offers escape from "the rack of thought," the tortures of trying to come to terms with life by relying solely on reason, unaided by religious faith. In the second half of the stanza, Maurice contemplates suicide, but life, or, more specifically, a faith in life and in himself, pulls him back, returning him to consciousness and an acceptance of life and himself. The shocking equation between religion and suicide that this stanza sets up reflects Clarke's view that both are forms of escape, requiring a surrender of man's reason and self-worth. Maurice is drawn to both kinds of withdrawal, and he recovers his sanity only when he is able to reject both.

Maurice takes a significant step in this direction in the ninth section of the poem, in which he begins to think of man not as fallen and inherently sinful, but as essentially good and free to enjoy the pleasures of life. Maurice's first hazy grasp of this notion comes through an Edenic vision that contrasts sharply with his dream of suicide earlier in the poem, and calls to mind the experience of the pilgrims in "Wandering Men" (*Pilgrimage*). Maurice is lying awake at night, listening to the talk of some warders, when the vision comes:

Maurice lay listening to their talk of sport.
One night they climbed to the Robbers' Cave
Beyond Kilmainham, above the coach-road.
Often he heard them repeating a tale
Of the Gate, the Garden and the Fountain:
Three words that lulled him as he fell
Asleep: Mesopotamian sound
Of a claustral stream that stelled him.

The words became mysterious
With balsam, fragrance, banyan trees,
Forgetting the ancient law of tears,
He dreamed in the desert, a league from Eden.
How could he pass the Gate, the sworded
Seraphim, find the primal Garden,
The Fountain? He had but three words
And all the summer maze was guarded.

                                    (*CP*, 340)

The gate that will open the portals of St. Patrick's Hospital is that
which leads into "the primal Garden" of a state of mind that denies
original sin and all that follows from it. Maurice needs to discover his
own Edenic being, just as the pilgrims of "Wandering Men" did, and
to forget "the ancient law of tears" of his religious upbringing.

Maurice's vision also indicates that art has a part to play in his
recovery, similar to the role accorded it in "The Loss of Strength" and
"Forget Me Not." (The lost Mnemosyne of the poem's title was both a
Greek goddess of memory and the mother of the nine Muses.) These
two stanzas emphasize the power of language and the imagination to
create new realities markedly different from the repressive religious
world that has led to Maurice's illness. The sound of "The Gate, the
Garden and the Fountain" mesmerizes Maurice, and in the second
stanza, these words become "mysterious," conjuring up exotic and
sensual images of "balsam, fragrance, and banyan trees." These stan-
zas also demonstrate, through sound patterns, the creative force of
language. The internal off-rhyme between "lulled" and "fell," and the
dominant liquid "l" sound in "three words that lulled him as he fell /
Asleep," are meant to affect the reader in much the same way that
Maurice is affected by "the Gate, the Garden and the Fountain"; this

hypnotic feeling is heightened in the closing lines of the stanza, in which the "l" sounds are brought together with "s" sounds, culminating in the final onomatopoeic "stelled."[8]

Once Maurice sees, through the symbols of the Gate, Garden, and Fountain, that his return to sanity depends on accepting his own worth and freeing himself from the effects of religious prohibition, his recovery proceeds steadily. In section eleven, he breaks a long fast by eating a dish of strawberries. The brief following section (originally published in *Flight to Africa* under the title "Fragaria") sets that action in the larger context of Maurice's struggle against guilt and self-doubt:

> Nature
> Remembering a young believer
> And knowing his weakness
> Could never stand to reason
> Gave him from the lovely hand
> Of his despairing mother,
> A dish of strawberries
> To tempt
> And humble the fast
> That had laid him nearer than they were
> Along her clay.
>
> (*CP*, 344)

Nature works here in opposition to Maurice's religion. Maurice was once a "young believer" in Nature and all that it stands for, and Nature knows that Maurice's "weakness"—literally his weakness from hunger, but also his mental condition and its cause—cannot "stand to reason." This phrase suggests both that Maurice's religious training makes no sense according to the dictates of reason, and that it cannot measure up to the power of reason and the humanistic assumptions embodied in it. In giving him the strawberries, Nature helps Maurice overcome his fast from life, the tendency toward self-denial that is a product of his religious heritage.

The final section of the poem describes Maurice's release from the hospital as a rebirth, in sharp contrast to the "death" of Maurice's entrance into the hospital recorded in the poem's opening section:

Rememorised, Maurice Devane
Went out, his future in every vein,
The Gate had opened. Down Steeven's Lane
The high wall of the Garden, to right
Of him, the Fountain with a horse-trough,
Illusions had become a story.
There was the departmental storey
Of Guinness's, God-given right
Of goodness in every barrel, tun,
They averaged. Upon that site
Of Watling Street and the Cornmarket,
At Number One in Thomas Street
Shone in the days of the ballad-sheet
The house in which his mother was born.

(*CP*, 351–352)

No longer obsessed with the guilt of his past, but carrying "his future in every vein," Maurice walks through the gate that had "closed with a clang" in section one, the gate leading away from religious prohibition and its effects and toward an awareness of self-worth. The poem ends, as it began, with an image of procreation, and the last line, "The house in which his mother was born," counterpoints the first of the poem, "Past the house where he was got." The difference between these two images, and between the language in which they are presented, marks the difference between Maurice as mentally ill and Maurice as healthy.

The imagery and movement of the poem's close also suggest this distinction. The darkness surrounding Maurice's conception in the poem's opening is replaced by the light illuminating his mother's birthplace. The deliberately stumbling rhythms and syntax of the poem's opening are countered by the slightly anapestic, almost lilting movement of the last two lines, and by a syntactical ordering that builds pleasurably from "upon that site" to the final emphasis on "the house in which his mother was born." The final line also suggests another act of being born that the poem has described—Maurice's rebirth. Having moved from the darkness of guilt and self-degradation to the light of confidence and self-esteem, Maurice has, by the poem's close, been born anew, or, to use Clarke's term, "rememorised."

Rather extravagant claims have been made for *Mnemosyne Lay in Dust*. When it first appeared, one reviewer hailed it as "the most important poem from any Irish poet in twenty years," arguing that it went as "far beyond the previous corpus of Mr. Clarke's poetic achievement as Beethoven's Ninth Symphony is beyond his preceding compositions."[9] An American critic called it "one of the important sequences of the century."[10] Other readers have seen the poem as a powerful allegory about alienated twentieth-century man.[11]

Such arguments have tended to overlook the connection between *Mnemosyne Lay in Dust* and Clarke's earlier work, particularly *Pilgrimage* and *Night and Morning*. And when the poem is read against the best of the earlier lyrics, judgments as to its place in Clarke's canon are likely to be tempered. For all its poetic variety and depth of portrayal, *Mnemosyne Lay in Dust* lacks the complexity of vision that informs poems such as "Tenebrae," "The Straying Student," "Martha Blake," and "Ancient Lights." These poems, while recognizing the need for the humanistic philosophy that returns Maurice to sanity, also acknowledge the limitations of that perspective, chiefly its inability to address man's spiritual needs. Although it may be argued that *Mnemosyne Lay in Dust*, by bringing the reader so close to its disturbed hero, offers a more thorough exploration of the effects of religious prohibition than do any of those earlier poems, Maurice's progression from darkness to light is ultimately too one-dimensional to be wholly convincing, too blind to the awful truth that, in the language of "Wandering Men," man needs *both* centaur and house of prayer and yet can never reconcile the two.

The critical acclaim for *Mnemosyne Lay in Dust* has also tended to blink at stylistic flaws that make it less successful than the best of Clarke's earlier lyrics. The excessive wordplay in the final stanza, for example, although it helps underscore the sense of release being described, suggests a jesting or ironic stance that is inappropriate to the poem's close. The confusion that this kind of writing can generate is perhaps most evident in several passages in section fifteen describing Maurice's fellow-patients. The reader confronted with a couplet such as "And Mr. Thornton, light-footed as the waves. / 'Cresh o' the waves,' he sings, 'cresh o' the waves' " (*CP*, 346) may well wonder how seriously these patients and their illnesses are being taken. And he can only regret the judgment that found it necessary, for the sake of *rime riche*, to follow the haunting description of Farrell the undertaker as "gliding to death in patent leather slippers" with the lame line, "His coffin was already on the slip" (*CP*, 347).

This is not, however, to argue that *Mnemosyne Lay in Dust* is an unimpressive poem. It stands without question as one of the major accomplishments of Clarke's later years, and shows him still willing and able to wrestle with the complex and profound issues that inform the best of his work, and that make him a poet who speaks to an audience far beyond the shores of his native Ireland.

8

"The Oracle, Not Yet Dumb" (II): Late Erotic Poems

The reader of Clarke can open the *Collected Poems* to almost any page and find some evidence of Clarke's lifelong concern with sexuality. But this interest took on a new intensity in the last years of Clarke's career, reflected in the great volume and variety of erotic verse appearing in *Flight to Africa* and the collections that followed it. In an introspective poem entitled "From a Diary of Dreams" (*Flight to Africa*), Clarke offers a justification for the erotic nature of much of his work:

> The under-mind is our semi-private part:
> Not senile lust but stirring of religion
> Long since abused, below in the pit of us.
> The goddess, striding naked, with prodigious
> Limbs—worn-out image—thrysis clad in ivy.
>
> (*CP*, 259)

For Clarke, the erotic is important in his poetry because it is important in human nature, and his eroticism, far from being merely the product of "senile lust," has the force of a religion "long since abused" by puritanical attitudes toward sexuality. If *Mnemosyne Lay in Dust* shows what happens when man, misled by these attitudes, tries to ignore the "goddess, striding naked," Clarke's erotic poetry shows what happens when he accepts her. And it does so chiefly by trying to convey erotic experience and, through that experience, Clarke's humanistic belief in man's right to enjoy the pleasures of life, the erotic included.

114

Eroticism takes a wide variety of forms in Clarke's late poetry. It includes, for example, the suggestive seductiveness of "Anacreontic" (*A Sermon on Swift*, 1968):

> They say that Byron, though lame
> In the wrong foot, danced the Sir Roger
> To the old-fashioned tune of De Coverly
> With Lady Caroline Lamb.
> But others had done the same.
> The middle-aged banker, Sam Rogers
> Twice shared a covering letter
> With her. But O when she'd seen the
> Translator of Anacreon,
> Young Thomas Moore in the wax-light,
> Step to her bed without shame,
> A naked Cupid, all rosy,
> All roundy, no epicene
> Lisping in anapaestics,
> Softly she blew out the flame-tip,
> Glimmered in white, as the moon rose,
> And unpetalled the rose-bud from Paestum.
>
> (*CP*, 482)

The erotic force of this poem depends partly on syntax, specifically the way in which the one long sentence that describes the sexual encounter between Thomas Moore and Lady Caroline Lamb alluringly delays the final action until the last line. Also, the striking final metaphor, suggestively cloaking Lady Caroline's sexual surrender in a comparison with a rose-bud losing its petals, heightens the erotic effect. The reference to Paestum, a city in ancient Greece where the soil produced roses that bloomed twice a year, steers the metaphor away from cliché at the same time that it brings the poem to a close on an appropriately Greek note. (Moore translated Anacreon, the ancient Greek poet famous for his erotic verse.)

A very different kind of eroticism appears in "Phallomeda" (*The Echo at Coole*, 1968), which mixes explicit sexual description with rough, bawdy humor. The story of the poem, taken from Gaelic literary tradition,[1] centers around Dagda, one of the ancient Irish gods known as the Tuatha de Danaan. In the Gaelic version of the tale, Dagda, known far and wide for his tremendous appetite, is sent to

scout an enemy camp during a war; once there, he is detained by
being fed an enormous quantity of porridge and then delivered into
the hands of a beautiful woman (the daughter of Dagda's enemy in the
original, a Greek goddess in Clarke's version). Clarke's description of
the sexual encounter between Dagda and the goddess is characteristi-
cally overt and purposefully mirthful:

> His stomach was bulging out with gusto
> Below her bosom, but his lust
> Held him in bonds, he could not burst from.
> > He clasped her, toppled off,
> Rolled over with a double bound
> Impatiently trying to mount himself
> But was unable to rebound:
> > The goddess was on top.
>
> She budded with hope on that mighty paunch,
> Pink, white, as he grabbed her by the haunches
> So hard that she was scarcely conscious:
> > Bonnie bush out of reach.
> Then, side by side, they sank. She fumbled
> To fire his godhead while he clumsied,
> Till she could hear the porridge mumble,
> > Slapdash as foreign speech.
>
> > > (CP, 454)

The reason for the poem's coarse humor and explicitness is explained
in the final stanza:

> So in the words of the Great Mahaffy,
> Annalists frolicked with the pen and laughed
> At what they saw in the Hereafter,
> > Forgetting their horn-beads.
> Anticipating Rabelais,
> They wrote of the god who lay
> With loveliness. I copy that lay,
> > Applaud their disobedience.
>
> > > (CP, 455)

The medieval Irish monks who transcribed the pagan tale of Dagda
are seen here as enjoying, largely because of the story's explicit
humor, a momentary freedom from their ascetic religious discipline.

This is precisely the effect that Clarke, through the humor in his version of the story, is trying to work on the reader.

The long narrative poems that Clarke wrote near the end of his life, based on classical and Irish legend, represent his most concerted effort to convey erotic experience. Two of these, "The Dilemma of Iphis" (*Orphide*, 1970) and *Tiresias* (1971), take their stories from Ovid's *Metamorphoses*, and in them Clarke uses the flexibility of the hexameter, the classical measure usually reserved by the Greeks and Romans for epic or didactic poetry, to achieve extremely erotic effects. An example is this passage from "The Dilemma of Iphis," in which Iphis, on the eve of her marriage, daydreams about the rape of Leda:

> Bluster of wing-clap above her frightened
> Leda, who was two days pregnant, as she bathed in the local
>   river.
> Surprised by a swan, she forgot her obedience to Tyndarus,
> Her dutiful Spartan husband, as floating, sustained by the
>   web-feet,
> Hover of wing-tips, breathlessly, she rose and dipped with
> The god who had hidden excess of his solar rays in the simple
> Whiteness of a swan. Hour long conjoined, she drenched,
>   undrenched him
> Until his tail-feathers drooped.
>
>   (*CP*, 503)

Here Clarke uses the rhythmic variety permitted by his loose hexameter line to bring the reader as close as possible to Leda's experience. The series of interruptions—"floating, sustained by the web-feet, / Hover of wing-tips, breathlessly"—mirrors the pleasurable delays in the sexual act being described by holding off the reader's expectation of syntactical fulfillment. And when that fulfillment comes, it rocks with the suggestive rhythm of "she rose and dipped with." The final sentence ends abruptly, as does the rape, landing on the appropriately unromantic word "drooped."

The obscene *double entendre* in the last line anchors the description in the physical, reminding the reader that the poem is concerned not with romanticized or mythologized sexuality, but with human sexuality. Yeats's "Leda and the Swan" offers a useful point of comparison here. Yeats, whose interest in this event is much more cosmic and mythic than is Clarke's, emphasizes the strength and mystery of the swan ("A sudden blow: the great wings beating still") and the helplessness of the victim ("Above the staggering girl"). Clarke's purpose, on the other hand, is essentially erotic, and so he quickly shifts his focus from the bird to Leda and the pleasure that she gets from the experience. Moreover, by the end of the passage, Clarke's Leda has become the sexual aggressor, whereas Yeats's Leda remains passive. However, Clarke's treatment is not necessarily any less broad in its implications than is Yeat's; the very insistence on detail and on the nonmythic aspects of the rape contributes to the poem's ultimate transcendence of the event by conveying a sexual experience that makes a poetic argument for the importance of the erotic in human nature.

This principle of conveying erotic experience in the interest of celebrating man's sexual nature is also evident in *Tiresias*. This poem considerably dilates Ovid's brief account of the prophet Tiresias, who experienced both male and female sexuality, and who, in Clarke's version, emerges as a convincing spokesman for the erotic:

> . . . I attended once the
> Eleusinian Mysteries. Fragrant myrtling in forest
> Groves, kettling, lightly-fingered flute, danced procession
> Flaring from temple-steps, women undoing calyptra.
> I, too, leaped among the hair-pin scatterers, divesting
> Themselves for the limb-gleaming whirlabout of maenadic
> Love-embrace. Broached, lined, by the vine-men, I sank
>   through the last
> Shudder of bliss into the Divine.
>
> (CP, 535)

Clarke uses in *Tiresias* some of the same techniques observed in "The Dilemma of Iphis" to convey the bliss of sexual relations, but often for a different effect. A passage describing Pyrrha (Tiresias as a woman) and her student-shepherd lover, Chelos, provides an example:

> . . . And so we had supper,
> Sharing a skin of Aetnian wine until the midnight
> Hour, then tiptoed tipsily back to our mantled love-bed.
> Drowsily entwined, we moved slowly, softly, withholding
> Ourselves in sweet delays until at last we yielded,

> Mingling our natural flow, feeling it almost linger
> Into our sleep.
>
> (*CP*, 522)

Here alliteration and internal vowel harmonies such as those between "slowly" and "witholding," "sweet" and "yielded," and "mingling" and "linger" help convey a tenderness missing from the description of Leda and the swan. Also the passage ends not with a sudden drooping of tail-feathers but with a fading into sleep, a movement echoed rhythmically by the series of participial phrases that slowly and suggestively bring the final sentence to its conclusion.

Unfortunately, such poetic celebrations of the erotic are occasionally offset in Clarke's late narrative poems by passages that betray a desire chiefly to shock his audience, rather than pay homage to human sexuality. In these passages, erotic material is introduced with little or no justification, and description fails to rise above the level of clinical detail. An example from "The Dilemma of Iphis" is this account of Telethusa, Iphis's mother, after she is visited in the night by a goddess:

> The portent was gone. In her trouble,
> In her joy, Telethusa got up and knelt on the chilled stone-floor,
> Thanking our Lady of Pharos, then dragged herself, slowly,
>   wearied,
> Back to the bed and warmed her great belly against her
>   husband's
> Thighs as he turned to her in his slumber, feeling his penis
> Stir up, inflamed by her nearness.
>
> (*CP*, 501)

When Clarke turned to the Irish literary past for erotic material, he found a tradition at least as rich as that represented by Ovid. Moreover, one of the hallmarks of Gaelic literature is its emphasis on the physical and concrete, and Gaelic writing dealing with sexual matters is no exception. This specificity suited Clarke's purposes and style perfectly, as can be seen in "The Healing of Mis" (*Orphide*, 1970). This poem, based on an ancient Irish tale entitled *The Romance of Mis and Dubh Ruis*,[2] tells of the daughter of the King of Munster in the days of Fionn. According to the story, the daughter, stricken with grief when her father is killed in battle, drinks his blood and goes mad. She flees to the remote glens and peaks of the mountain in

County Kerry that still bears her name, Slieve Mish, and lives there as a wild creature for three centuries. In the ninth century, a harper named Dubh Ruis accepts an offer from the King of Munster to try to bring her back to civilization, and he does so by seducing her.

The original Gaelic tale leaves little to the imagination in its description of how the harper tempts Mis: he spreads his cloak in the shade of a tree, takes out his harp, and, last but not least, opens his trousers and bares himself. In a few minutes, Mis discovers him:

> As she looked at him, she caught sight of his nakedness and his members of pleasure. "What are those?" she said, pointing to his bag or his eggs—and he told her. "What is this?" said she about the other thing which she saw. "That is the wand of the feat," said he. "I do not remember that," said she, "my father hadn't anything like that. The wand of the feat; what is the feat?" "Sit beside me," said he, "and I will do the feat of the wand for you." "I will," said she, "and stay you with me." "I will," said he, and lay with her and knew her, and she said, "Ha, ba, ba, that was a good feat; do it again." "I will," said he; "however, I will play the harp for you first." "Don't mind the harp," said she, "but do the feat."[3]

The Gaelic tale also agrees with Clarke's view of sexuality as a natural and healthy aspect of human nature: "He thought that if he could lie with her and know her, it would be a good means and device for bringing her to her sense or her natural reason."[4] The parallel between Mis and Clarke's Maurice Devane of *Mnemosyne Lay in Dust* is worth noting; in another poem with Maurice as protagonist, "A Student in Paris" (*Old-Fashioned Pilgrimage*), Clarke sums up Maurice's numerous experiences in Paris brothels with the line: "The law of natural pleasure saned him" (*CP*, 385).

Clarke's version of the encounter between Mis and Dubh reproduces the original's detailed frankness, and also demonstrates Clarke's ability to convey erotic experience through rhythm, sound, and diction:

>   . . . Duv Ruis rested awhile in a sun-scented
> Vale, then hastened to spread his travelling cloak in the shade
>   Of a blossoming quicken-tree, tossed his ring-coins up,
> A silver and golden frolic of profit-making pelf,
>   Then arranged them carefully in emblems
> Along the cloth-edge, lay on his back to greet the Geilt
>   Opened his flap, exposed himself.

Holding his harp, the consolation of his bosom,
    He played a suantree with grace-notes that enspelled
Traditional tunes and, smiling quietly at his ruse,
    Waited. Soon his senses knew that loneliness
Stood by, a bareness modestly draped in tangle-black hair,
    With timeless hands, listening to the special
Melling that drew and soothed her mind as she stared
    In surmise at his rising flesh.

'Are you a man?' she asked. 'I am.' 'What's that you are holding?'
    'A harp.' 'I remember the triangle.' 'Pluck it.'
'You will not harm me?' 'I won't.' She tapped the
    sounding-board,
    Laughed as it answered her. 'What's this I'm touching
Below?' 'A couple of pouched eggs I like to carry.'
    'Can you lay them as the poult-hen?' 'Only the glair.'
'What's this so high and mighty?' 'Marry-come-up, my dear:
    The wand of the feat as scholars declare!'

                            (*CP*, 511)

The abruptness of the last line in the first stanza brings the leisurely description of the harper's preparations to a deliberately emphatic end. In the next stanza, as Mis approaches, internal vowel harmonies underscore Mis's mood ("melling that *drew* and *sooth*ed her mind") and her curiosity ("in sur*mise* at his *ris*ing flesh"). The dialogue depends largely on suggestive diction for its effect; phrases such as "a couple of pouched eggs," "the glair," and "the wand of the feat" raise the passage above the level of clinical detail used, for example, to describe Telethusa in bed with her husband in "The Dilemma of Iphis."

Much of the effectiveness of "The Healing of Mis" depends on the richness of its sound patterns, appropriately based on Gaelic models. An example is this description of Dubh Ruis bathing Mis, a passage that energetically celebrates the physical:

        . . . He sloshed
Himself as he lathered her down, soaped the skin of her back
With a lump of deer-fat, washed the crack between the slurried
    Cheeks, like a mother, turned her round, picked crabs from
Her sporran, nit-nurseries hidden in tiny flurries
    Through tangled tresses, then began

All over again. He soaped her body, washed it down,
    Drawing the wad of deer-skin to-and-fro
Softly between her glossing thighs, turned her around
    And frizzled her neglected faddle, noticed
It needed a thorough-going cleansing inside and out, scrubbed
    And douched it, cursing her ignorance, lack of care,
Then coiled her tresses neatly after he currycombed them
    As if she was a gainly mare.

                                                    (*CP*, 512–513)

Here terminal echoes such as those between "her *back*" and "*crabs* from" and "*slur*ried" and "*flur*ries" are reinforced by numerous internal harmonies: "*lath*ered" anticipates "her *back*," and is echoed later in "deer-*fat*" and "*crack*"; "*slur*ried" and "*flur*ries" find medial echoes in "turned" and "nit-*nurs*eries." This constant echoing across lines generates a verbal energy that contributes significantly to the passage's celebration of the flesh.

Passages such as this offer convincing evidence of the power of Clarke's late erotic poetry to argue appealingly for sexual inhibition and freedom. Nevertheless, comparison of these poems with the erotic verse in *Pilgrimage* and *Night and Morning* reveals their limitations: they celebrate the erotic, but usually in a vacuum, paying little heed to the forces, religious and social, ranged against an uninhibited acceptance of the pleasures of sexuality. Clarke's earlier poetry treating sexual passion is erotic precisely because it does recognize these forces. An example is this description of Nial and Gormlai, the lovers of "The Confession of Queen Gormlai" (*Pilgrimage*):

                For drizzling miles we kissed,
                We clung to the glistening saddle
                On roads that rang and misted
                Below us, promised madly
                To pray, but in cold heather
                We broke the marriage ring,
                Under your leathern cloak,
                By thoughts that were a sin.
                                        (*CP*, 160)

This stanza owes much of its effect to the tension between the uncontrollable feelings of Nial and Gormlai and the strictly controlled form used to describe them. The formal stanza and intricate patterns of assonance struggle to contain the unlawful passion of the lovers, functioning as a poetic expression of the social and religious mores that would condemn them. This tension gives the feelings of the lovers a force that they would not have alone. Clarke's late erotic poetry tends to lack this tension and complexity, just as *Mnemosyne Lay in Dust* lacks the profound ambivalence of poems such as "Tenebrae" and "The Straying Student," and just as Clarke's public poems, by converting complex private struggles into one-sided attacks on outward manifestations of repressive religious and social views, fall short of the depth and force of the earlier work.

No argument along this line is more compelling than a comparison of two Clarke love-making scenes, one late and one early: the affair of Chelos and Pyrrha in *Tiresias*, and the description of the young woman of Beare with her "big-booted captain" in "The Young Woman of Beare" (*Pilgrimage*). The *Tiresias* passage is typical of Clarke's later uninhibited style:

> Chelos lay asprawl and I knew that he must be dreaming of me
> For he murmured 'Pyrrha'. I fondled his ithyphallus, uncapped
>   it,
> Saw for the first time the knob, a purple-red plum, yet firmer.
> Covering him like a man, I moved until he gripped me:
> Faster, yet faster, we sped, determined down-thrust rivalling
> Up-thrust—succus glissading us—exquisite spasm
> Contracting, dilating, changed into minute preparatory
> Orgasms, a pleasure unknown to man, that culminated
> Within their narrowing circles into the great orgasmos.
>
> (CP, 522)

This is indisputably erotic, particularly in its imitative rhythms. But it is also, in places, crudely clinical, and it lacks the tensions of a larger context. In the passage from "The Young Woman of Beare" (discussed in chapter three), much is said by indirection and metaphor, and everything is said within the bounds of a tightly controlled line and a formal stanza, suggesting the tension between eroticism and asceticism that underlies the passage and the poem. The result is a piece of writing that is considerably more erotic than the *Tiresias* passage:

> Heavily on his elbow,
> He turns from a caress
> To see—as my arms open—

The red spurs of my breast.
I draw fair pleats around me
And stay his eye at pleasure,
Show but a white knee-cap
Or an immodest smile—
Until his sudden hand
Has dared the silks that bind me.

See! See, as from a lathe
My polished body turning!
He bares me at the waist
And now blue clothes uncurl
Upon white haunch. I let
The last bright stitch fall down
For him as I lean back,
Straining with longer arms
Above my head to snap
The silver knots of sleep.

(*CP*, 165)

Such a comparison is not meant to deny the genuine achievement of Clarke's late erotic verse. Described with great invention and energy, and loving without restraint, characters like Iphis, Pyrrha, and Mis celebrate human sexuality in an atmosphere of uninhibited joy and license, and so stand as important figures in Clarke's lifelong struggle to assert man's inherent right to encounter without shame or guilt that "goddess, striding naked," and to enjoy all the pleasures of this life.

9

"The Oracle, Not Yet Dumb" (III):
Gaelic Translations

No poet in the twentieth century was so deeply or so knowledgeably committed to the Irish tradition as was Austin Clarke. Coming of age during the years of the Irish literary revival, Clarke inherited a sense of the Irish cultural past from Yeats and his colleagues, but, unlike many Irish writers, including Yeats, Clarke remained dedicated throughout his life to what Augustine Martin has called "the ideal of an indigenous Irish art."[1] That ideal informs almost everything that Clarke wrote, but in many ways his commitment found its most successful expression in several groups of poems published in *Flight to Africa* and *The Echo at Coole*. In these free translations from the Gaelic, Clarke was able not only to express the spirit and poetic characteristics of Gaelic literature, but also to present convincingly the humanistic vision that is at the center of his work.

One of the most impressive of Clarke's efforts in this vein is "Mabel Kelly," one of a group of poems published in *Flight to Africa* under the heading of "Eighteenth Century Harp Songs," and based on poems by the Irish harpist and composer Turlough O'Carolan (1670–1738):

> Lucky the husband
> Who puts his hand beneath her head.
> They kiss without scandal
> Happiest two near feather-bed.
> He sees the tumble of brown hair

Unplait, the breasts, pointed and bare
    When nightdress shows
    From dimple to toe-nail,
All Mabel glowing in it, here, there, everywhere.

    Music might listen
    To her least whisper,
Learn every note, for all are true.
    While she is speaking,
    Her voice goes sweetly
To charm the herons in their musing.
Her eyes are modest, blue, their darkness
Small rooms of thought, but when they sparkle
    Upon a feast-day,
    Glasses are meeting,
Each raised to Mabel Kelly, our toast and darling.

Gone now are many Irish ladies
Who kissed and fondled, their very pet-names
Forgotten, their tibia degraded.
She takes their sky. Her smile is famed.
Her praise is scored by quill and pencil.
    Harp and spinet
    Are in her debt
And when she plays or sings, melody is content.

    No man who sees her
    Will feel uneasy.
He goes his way, head high, however tired.
    Lamp loses light
    When placed beside her.
She is the pearl and being of all Ireland
Foot, hand, eye, mouth, breast, thigh and instep,
    all that we desire.
Tresses that pass small curls as if to touch the ground;
    So many prizes
    Are not divided
Her beauty is her own and she is not proud.[2]

                (*CP*, 295–296)

The most immediately striking thing about this poem is its rhythmic complexity and energy. Although some of this is indebted to the considerable achievements of O'Carolan, Clarke's version goes significantly beyond its model, especially in its use of assonantal patterns.[3] In the first three lines, for example, the iambic rhythm that is the norm of the poem is thrown off by the trochaic inversion in the first line and the substitution of an anapest in the third, but also by the alteration of the syllable that carries the terminal echo (hus*band*" and "*scan*dal"). In the third stanza, the four stressed syllables of "She takes their sky. Her smile is famed" are arranged in an *abba* pattern of internal assonance. Moreover, "takes" and "fame" find an echo in "praise" in the following line, which concludes with the harmony between "quill" and "pen*cil*," subdued because the second half of the echo falls on an unstressed syllable. And finally, the terminal cross-assonance between "*pen*cil" and "con*tent*" ties the passage together while it underscores the rhythmic differences between the fifth line and the last line.

The advantage that Clarke gains from such techniques can be seen by comparing "Mabel Kelly" with George Sigerson's version of the same poem. Sigerson, an influential figure in the Irish literary revival and a man whom Clarke admired,[4] aimed at preserving O'Carolan's original meter, but he loses O'Carolan's rhythmic energy and irregularity. His version of the second stanza demonstrates this:

> No song the sweetest,
> No music meetest,
> But she sings its melody, full, soft, and true;
> Her cheek the rose a-blowing,
> With comrade lily glowing,
> Her glancing eyes, like opening blossoms blue.
> And a bard has sung how herons keen
> On hearing her victor-voice slumber serene.
> Her eyes of splendour
> Are wells of candour.—
> Here's thy health, go leór, a stór, our beauty bright queen![5]

The singsong quality, partly the result of the frequent feminine rhyme, does considerable violence to the irregular rhythms that distinguish O'Carolan's original.[6] Clarke's second stanza, on the other hand, by relying on assonantal links and by occasionally shifting the syllable that carries the echo, avoids this effect. It also stays much closer to the original, which relies principally on assonance.

The complex rhythms and subtle sound effects only partly explain the attraction of Clarke's "Mabel Kelly," however. The tenderness and intimacy that the poem conveys depend significantly on the attention paid to concrete details and the way in which they are juxtaposed with more general description. In the first stanza, the "tumble of brown hair / Unplait" and "the breasts, pointed and bare" and followed by a much less explicit description that moves steadily away from specific detail. The combination produces an image that is specific without being merely clinical and suggestive without being vapid. Similarly, the last stanza moves from extremely general comparisons—"Lamp loses light / When placed beside her" and "She is the pearl and being of all Ireland"—to the catalogue of Mabel's bodily parts (a catalogue that embroiders on O'Carolan considerably[7]).

These descriptions are obviously erotic, and the eroticism has a point to make. As Donald Davie has argued, "Mabel Kelly" reminds the reader that Gaelic and Catholic Ireland once enjoyed a period far less prudish and puritanical than the Ireland of Clarke's century.[8] Clarke's exploration of seventeenth- and eighteenth-century Gaelic culture throughout *Flight to Africa* and *The Echo at Coole* makes this point. As was seen in poems such as "The Lucky Coin" and "Three Poems About Children (I)," Clarke celebrated this period of Gaelic culture as an age in which secular life was not lived under the thumb of a powerful and repressive Irish Catholic Church. In Clarke's view, the Catholic Gael of this time, although his culture was in ruins and his religion in disrepute, still felt free to enjoy himself. "Poverty drew lip down," Clarke says in "Vanishing Irish" (*Ancient Lights*), "and yet there was laughter / In that raggedness of ours" (*CP*, 204). Clarke's effort to convey those qualities in his Gaelic translations parallels his celebration of sexuality in the late erotic poems and his argument for the humanistic vision that saves Maurice Devane in *Mnemosyne Lay in Dust*.

Clarke's most energetic expression of that Gaelic laughter is "O'Rourke's Feast" (*Flight to Africa*), a rendering of a Gaelic poem written by a contemporary of O'Carolan's, Hugh MacGauran, and describing a traditional Christmas festival in the castle of a sixteenth-century Irish chieftain.[9] In his version, Clarke uses the twelve-line stanza of the original and a pattern of terminal assonance that follows MacGauran closely:

Let O'Rourke's great feast be remembered by those
Who were at it, are gone, or not yet begotten.
A hundred and forty hogs, heifers and ewes
Were basting each plentiful day and gallons of pot-still
Poured folderols into the mugs. Unmarried
And married were gathering early for pleasure and sport.
'Your clay pipe is broken.' 'My pocket picked.' 'Your hat
Has been stolen.' 'My breeches lost.' 'Look at my skirt torn.'
'And where are those fellows who went half under my mantle
And burst my two garters?' 'Sure, no one's the wiser.'
'Strike up the strings again,' 'Play us a planxty.'
'My snuff-box, Annie, and now a double sizer.'

(*CP*, 300)

Comparison with Jonathan Swift's more famous version shows
how the form of Clarke's poem helps keep the point of view sym-
pathetic to the culture being described:

O'Rourke's noble fare
    Will ne'er be forgot,
By those who were there,
    Or those who were not.

His revels to keep,
    We sup and we dine
On seven score sheep,
    Fat bullocks, and swine.

Usquebaugh to our feast
    In pails was brought up,
A hundred at least,
    And a madder our cup.

O there is sport!
    We rise with the light
In disorderly sort,
    From snoring all night.

O how was I trick'd!
    My pipe it was broke,
My pocket was pick'd,
    I lost my new cloak.

> I'm rifled, quoth Nell,
>   Of mantle and kercher,
> Why then fare them well,
>   The de'el take the searcher.
>
> Come, harper, strike up;
>   But, first, by your favour,
> Boy, give us a cup:
>   Ah! this hath some savour.[10]

Despite this poem's considerable vigor, its alien stanza and meter tend to produce the mocking tone that Clarke's poem avoids. The light, swinging rhythms and frequent rhymes of Swift's version often insist on a distance between the poem's speaker and its subject, and the resultant note of irony betrays the hand of an outsider looking on with amusement at the bizarre antics of another race. Clarke himself took Swift to task for this, saying that in writing "The Description of an Irish Feast," Swift "became, by what may be called a by-blow, the Father of the Stage Irishman."[11]

In terms of sheer technique, Clarke's Gaelic translations rank high in his canon. Perhaps the most dazzling display of Clarke's ability to reproduce in English verse the intricate rhythms and sound patterns of Gaelic poetry is "Song of the Books" (*Flight to Africa*), a poem celebrating the Gaelic scholars and poets who struggled to keep the Irish tradition alive during the seventeenth and eighteenth centuries. The Gaelic bards that came to prominence at this time differed from the classical school of filés, which died out with the collapse of the Gaelic aristocracy in the seventeenth century, principally in their use of assonance and accentual song meters, and Clarke's poem follows its original, written by a nineteenth-century County Kerry schoolteacher named Tomás Ruadh O'Sullivan, in paying homage to these poets in their own mode.[12]

The poem opens with a description of a storm in the southwest of Ireland:

> South-westerly gale fiddled in rigging;
> Furled canvases in foam-clap, twigged
> The pulley-blocks. Billows were bigger.
>   The clouds fell out.
> In Madmen's Glen, snipe hit the grasses,

Rains in Tralee had towned their phantoms
While rocks were thrumming in the passes.
   Below a shout
Was whisper and among the boulders
   The frightened trout
Were hiding from the beaten coldness.
   Soon every snout
Was gone. The noises of new shingle
Along the coast had swept the Kingdom
Of Kerry, league by league, from Dingle
   In whirlabout.

                 (*CP*, 310)

The energy of this passage owes much to the inventiveness of Clarke's language, especially the vigorous verbs. But it also depends on the intricate sound patterns that run through each of the three triplets. In the first of these, "*fid*dled" anticipates the terminal echo that connects the three lines, and its sound carries over into the next line through the alliteration with "furled" and "foamclap." The second line reverberates with the internal harmony between "*can*vases" and "foam-*clap*." The third line echoes the second through "*bil*lows," which chimes with "twigged" at the same time that it looks forward to "*big*ger." The third line also is marked by the alliteration between "pulley-blocks," "billows," and "bigger." Each triplet displays this kind of intricacy, and the stanza as a whole is held together by the spinal rhyme between the short lines. O'Sullivan's poem has precisely the same stanzaic structure, and also uses terminal and internal assonance in each triplet and a spinal rhyme between the short lines.[13] (In fact, all eleven stanzas of the original share the same rhyme.)

    Within the bounds of such a rigid form, Clarke is able to achieve a remarkable variety of tone. In its celebration of the eighteenth-century Irish bard Owen Roe O'Sullivan, "Song of the Books" takes on a rugged, no-holds-barred voice appropriate to O'Sullivan, a man whom Daniel Corkery describes as "a wastrel with loud laugh":[14]

Lightly, Red-head O'Sullivan
Who fought with Rodney, jolly jacktar
Too much at sea, thin as a marlin
   Spike, came and went,

> Poet, schoolmaster, parish clerk.
> He drank his Bible money at Mass-time,
> A moll upon his knee, bare-arsed.
>
> (*CP*, 314)

In the next stanza, the tone changes radically, as Clarke honors the Aisling, a standard form for Irish poets in O'Sullivan's day, and one that Clarke himself used as a model.[15] The Aisling was a vision poem, and usually opened with the poet falling asleep and waking in an idyllic natural setting; the quiet mood of this genre is reflected in the quality of Clarke's description of it:

> At dawn, in a wood of sorrel, branchy
> Dew-droppy, where sunlight gilded sapling
> And silvered holly, or by the bank
>   Of Brosna, Moy,
> Our poets saw a woman smiling.
> Her tresses, bright as celandine,
> Could not conceal her pure white side,
>   Was she from Troy?
> Or was she Venus whose fondled breast
>   Could never cloy?
>
> (*CP*, 315)

In "Beyond the Pale" (*Flight to Africa*), a long semi-meditative poem recounting a journey through Ireland that Clarke made with his second wife, Nora, Clarke concludes with a vision of Ireland that expresses his commitment to his cultural past:

> At Gallerus, the pale Atlantic rages.
> Bad weather, hard times, known to the Ancient Crow
> Of Achill, flapping out of the earth-brown pages
> Of manuscripts, the Stag of Leiterlone
> Uncragging, Fintan, half-way to transmigration,
> A roaming salmon, where billows dredge the shingle.
>
> Now, after a century of rags, young girl
> With skin the insolent have fondled, Earl
> And settler in his turn, the Hag of Dingle
> Is stretching. Eire, clamant with piety,
> Remembering the old mythology.
>
> (*CP*, 293)

No Irish poet in this century believed more passionately in "Remembering the old mythology" than did Clarke—be it the pagan mythology of the "Ancient Crow of Achill," the religious mythology of medieval Ireland, or the hedonistic mythology of the days when an Irish poet could drink "his Bible money at Mass-time / A moll upon his knee, bare-arsed." But Clarke's lifelong celebration of the Irish tradition has more than historical significance. In all his poetry, including the great variety of poems that he wrote in the last twelve years of his life, Clarke used his commitment to "the old mythology" to express his humanistic vision. Clarke's late poems carry on the struggle of morning against night—in psychological terms in poems such as *Mnemosyne Lay in Dust*, in erotic terms in poems such as "The Healing of Mis," and in historical terms in poems such as "O'Rourke's Feast." And because of this, they speak to a much wider audience than the specifically Irish one that Clarke seemed so determined to address.

Epilogue

A study of Austin Clarke's poetry might end as well as begin with Easter Monday, 1916. The events of that day, and the faith in an independent Irish state and culture that fueled them, left a mark on the young Clarke that can be traced from the first lines of *The Vengeance of Fionn* in 1917 to the last of "The Wooing of Becfola" in 1974. Indeed, Clarke's lifelong commitment to the ideal of an indigenous Irish art might be said to owe much to the Easter Rising and its spirit.

It also owed something to the inspiration of one of the men, also a poet, who led the Rising and whom Clarke, standing with Stephen MacKenna in front of the G.P.O. on Easter Monday, surely had in mind in thinking of "those friends who, as we knew, must be at their posts, so near to us or somewhere else in the city."[1] Thomas MacDonagh was, in fact, at his post just then, the rebel stronghold set up in Jacob's Biscuit Factory south of the Liffey. The son of an English mother and a conservative Irish father, MacDonagh had arrived at that post by way of Douglas Hyde's Gaelic League. At the age of thirty, he gave up a conventional teaching job to join Padraic Pearse in his unorthodox bilingual school at St. Enda's. The two men had much in common, particularly their interest in Gaelic culture; MacDonagh even translated several of Pearse's Irish poems into English, including one that proved tragically prophetic for both men:

> Naked I saw thee
>> O beauty of beauty!
> And I blinded my eyes
>> For fear I should flinch.

I heard thy music
  O melody of melody!
And I shut my ears
  For fear I should fail.

I kissed thy lips,
  O sweetness of sweetness!
And I hardened my heart
  For fear of my ruin.

I blinded my eyes,
  And my ears I shut,
I hardened my heart
  And my love I quenched.

I turned by back
  On the dream I had shaped,
And to this road before me
  My face I turned.

I set my face
  To the road here before me,
To the work that I see
  To the death that I shall get.[2]

By 1915, the year before the Rising, MacDonagh's interest in Gaelic culture had grown considerably, and he set his mind to "the work that I see," the cause of Irish independence, with all the zeal of a recent convert. In a letter written in May of that year, the intensity of his commitment, as well as the hand of Pearse, can be seen. "It is worth living in Ireland as one of the directors of the Irish Volunteers," he wrote. "Of course, none but the best metal has stood the test . . . those who under all circumstances and at all times must and will be Irish rebels. Zealous martyrs and so saviors and liberators, for I am confident we shall win this time, through peace, I hope, but if necessary by war."[3]

Clarke met MacDonagh about this time at University College, Dublin, where MacDonagh had secured a post as lecturer in English. In the early months of 1916, Clarke attended a series of lectures that MacDonagh gave on Anglo-Irish literature. Clarke has recalled those days in *A Penny in the Clouds*:

Students watch their lecturers with close attention, so it was that late in the Spring of 1916, I began to realize, with a foreboding, that something was about to happen for I noticed at times, though only for a few seconds, how abstracted and worried Thomas MacDonagh looked. Suddenly, one day, during a lecture on the Young Ireland Poets, he took a large revolver from his pocket and laid it on the desk. "Ireland can only win freedom by force," he remarked, as if to himself.[4]

No long after, Ireland struck for her freedom with force, and Mac-Donagh's ominous prophecy in "Naked I saw thee . . ." came true; along with thirteen other rebels, including Pearse, MacDonagh was executed a few days after the Rising as a traitor to the British crown.

The university lectures that the Rising and MacDonagh's death had fatally interrupted were published a month later under the title of *Literature in Ireland: Studies Irish and Anglo-Irish*. In this book, MacDonagh argues for what he calls the Irish Mode, a literature that, although written in English, expresses the native culture. The artist who would write in this mode must, MacDonagh says, "speak not merely of his people, but to them and for them, discovering them to themselves, expressing them for themselves."[5]

MacDonagh's words describe precisely Clarke's work and aims. Clarke spoke *of* the Irish people almost exclusively, focusing insistently on things Irish, from the sweeping heroic tales of ancient times down to the most niggling affairs of contemporary Ireland; he spoke *to* the Irish people just as exclusively, addressing himself specifically to an Irish audience in a voice saturated with the sounds and rhythms of the native Gaelic tradition; and finally, he spoke *for* the Irish people in all his efforts to come to terms with forces—from the most profoundly held religious beliefs to the most crassly motivated political and social attitudes—that he saw as oppressive, spiritually and materially, to the people of Ireland.

And yet the central paradox of Clarke's work remains: for all its relentless pursuit of MacDonagh's dream, in the end it transcends any notion of an "Irish Mode." Behind the sensuality of the young woman of Beare lying in lust with her "big-booted captain," the sudden discoveries of the straying student "growing bold as light in Greece," the moment of illumination visited on the young Clarke standing in the doorway of the Black Church and marveling at the aftereffects of a summer shower, the scathing attack on an Irish

Catholic bishop who "declared / That flame-wrapped babes are spared / Our life-time of temptation," the painful struggles of Maurice Devane in a Dublin mental institution, the erotic experiences of the legendary Mis in the mountains of County Kerry, the laughter of a Gaelic nation faced with the raggedness of poverty and cultural distintegration—behind all these singularly Irish figures and events lies a humanistic vision that is arguing, with all the powers that an accomplished artist can bring to bear, for the dignity and worth of man.

It was no less an Irish separatist than Thomas MacDonagh who said: "The deeds of a few men who see clearly, who know surely, and who act definitely, count for much. We can be concentrated into a little clan; and he who makes music for his little clan makes music for all the world."[6] MacDonagh's comment might well stand as the last word on Austin Clarke, a man who devoted a lifetime to making music for "the little clan" of modern Ireland, but in the process created a body of poetry that, informed by a vision of a fuller and richer humanity, sings as well to all the world.

Appendix

Although *The Vengeance of Fionn* (1917) is usually cited as his first published poem, Clarke published four poems in a Dublin literary weekly entitled *New Ireland* in 1916 and early 1917. None of these poems has been reprinted, although the last, "In Doire Dha Bhoth," was revised slightly and used in *The Vengeance of Fionn* (see *Collected Poems*, pp. 26–27).

The Isle.—A Fantasy

The evening light is on the sea,
Goldenly! Goldenly!
The billows poise and slowly roll,
But the gleeful wavelets capriole
As the leaves upon a windward tree.

A-peep upon the blue sea verge,
Wrought by a wizened thaumaturge
A little magic island lies,
Fantasque with flowers and mulberries
And mottled cliffs above the surge.

Ah! sweetest, to that Isle we fled
One purpline night: thy lips were red
And laughing i' the lonely gloom,
Though bitterly the driven spume
Had stung them till they richly bled.

And as we lay there drowsily,
Mnemosyne! Mnemosyne!

A yellow star burnt in the air,
And strange bewailing shadows were
Adrift upon the angered sea.

> *New Ireland*, 8 July 1916, p. 349

Song

O Lightfoot Girl!
In the golden swirl
Of a sweet caprice, of a delicate whim,
You fly away
Like a bird off spray,
But you leave the loneliest sorrow with him
Who laughingly loves you, Lightfoot Girl!

O Lightfoot Girl!
The tiniest twirl
Of a whitely beckoning hand could wile
Your lover to speed
By valley and mead
To the wonderful waters that bluely enisle
The end of the world, O Lightfoot Girl!

> *New Ireland*, 22 July 1916, p. 381

A Memory

At some strange dawn, it may be, you will think
How soon the lilac-time of Youth forsook
The lonely golden vale; and how we shook
The Tree of Joy until the fruiting flowers
Fell prettily on us in purple showers.
How you would talk with daintily laughing ease
And weave the silver thread of repartees,
Or gravely we would make the world anew
And have all roses nor ever a twig of rue.
How from a grassy cape in June-time days
We saw the sun burn down in scarlet haze,
Green wavelets on the saffony sands arow
All delicately tripping on tiptoe,
And tiny stars upon the sky's blue brink.

> *New Ireland*, 19 Aug. 1916, p. 444

In Doire Dha Bhoth
A Fragment

Flower-quiet in the rush-strewn sheiling at the dawntime
    Grainne lay,
While beneath the birch-topped roof the sunlight groped upon
    its way,
And stooped above her sleeping white body with a wasp-yellow
    ray.
The hot breath of the day awoke her, and, weary of its heat,
She wandered out by noisy elms on the cool mossy peat,
Where the shadowed leaves, like pecking linnets, nodded
    around her feet.

She leaned and saw in the fawn-grey waters by twisted hazel
    boughs
Her lips like heavy drooping poppies in a rich redness drowse,
Then shallow-lightly touched the ripples until her wet lips were
Burning as ripened rowan berries through the white winter air.

Lazily she lingered, gazing so,
As the slender oziers where the waters flow,
As green twigs of sally swaying to and fro.

Sleepy moths fluttered in her dark eyes,
And her lips grew quieter than lullabies.
Swaying with the reedgrass over the stream,
Lazily she lingered, cradling a dream.

A brown bird rises out of the marshes,
By sallow pools flying on winds from the sea,
By pebbly rivers, tired of the salt gusts,
Sweetly 'twill whistle on a mountainy tree.
So, gladdened, impulsive, Grainne arising,
Sped through the bluebells under the branches,
White by the alders, glimmering, she
Stole in the shadows, flashing through sunshine,
Her feet like the raindrops on withered leaves falling, Lightful
    and free!

New Ireland, 17 Feb. 1917, p. 243

Notes

1. "The Literary Separatist": Introduction

1. *A Penny in the Clouds: More Memories of Ireland and England* (London: Routledge & Kegan Paul, 1968), pp. 31–32.

2. *Poetry in Modern Ireland* (Cork: Mercier Press, 1951), p. 42.

3. *The Course of Irish Verse in English* (New York: Sheed & Ward, 1947), p. 150.

4. "Irish Poetry To-Day," *The Dublin Magazine*, NS 10, No. 5 (Jan.–March 1935): 32.

5. Until 1961, Clarke's name was virtually unknown in critical circles outside Ireland. In that year, the Dublin publishing firm of Dolmen Press brought out a collection entitled *Later Poems*, which included all of Clarke's lyrics published in private editions between 1929 and 1960. The book was distributed in England and the United States by Oxford University Press, and earned Clarke an immediate reputation among connoisseurs of poetry. The reaction of the British poet Charles Tomlinson was, perhaps, the most dramatic: "To my mind, this is undoubtedly *the* literary event of 1961. . . . Clarke deserves the reputation of the most important Irish poet writing today" ("Poets and Mushrooms: A Retrospect of British Poetry in 1961," *Poetry* 100, No. 2 [1962]: 113).

In academic circles, Donald Davie, the English critic, called attention to Clarke's work as early as 1957, four years before *Later Poems* was published (review of *Ancient Lights: Poems and Satires*, *Irish Writing*, No. 34 [Spring 1956], pp. 57–58). In 1964, a book published in the United States entitled *Celtic Cross: Studies in Irish*

Culture and Literature (eds. Ray B. Browne et al. [Lafayette, Ind.: Purdue University Studies]) offered three critical essays arguing, with varying degrees of enthusiasm and detail, for the worth of Clarke's work: George Brandon Saul, "The Poetry of Austin Clarke" (pp. 26–38); Maurice Harmon, "The Later Poetry of Austin Clarke" (pp. 39–55); and William John Roscelli, "The Private Pilgrimage of Austin Clarke" (pp. 56–69). The following year, one of the most insightful pieces of criticism on Clarke, Augustine Martin's "The Rediscovery of Austin Clarke," appeared in an Irish journal (*Studies* 54, No. 216 [1965]: 408–434), and in 1972 and 1974, the *Times Literary Supplement* published long essays on Clarke ([Seamus Deane], review of *Tiresias: A Poem*, 1 Dec. 1972, pp. 1459–1460; and Martin Dodsworth, "To Forge the Irish Conscience," review of *Austin Clarke: Collected Poems*, 13 Dec. 1974, pp. 1406–1407). A book-length treatment of Clarke—Susan Halpern's *Austin Clarke, His Life and Works* (Dublin: Dolmen Press)—also appeared in 1974. *Austin Clarke: A Study of His Writings*, by G. Craig Tapping (Totowa, N.J.: Barnes & Noble, 1981), appeared too late to be taken into consideration in this study.

6. Donald Davie has made this point about Yeat's later work. Yeats's feelings of disappointment, so evident in the *Playboy* furor, were heightened by the political resistance that sprang up in 1913 to an offer on the part of Hugh Lane, Lady Gregory's nephew, to donate a collection of modern paintings to Dublin on the condition that a gallery be built by an English architect to house them. At this point, as Davie says, despite his continued efforts at the Abbey thereafter, his response to the Rising and its aftermath, and his service in the Irish Free State Senate in the 1920s, Yeats "had in certain important matters lost hope, and he withdrew in the second half of his life, out of the arena of national aspiration into himself, making his magnificent later poetry mainly personal, passionate and subjective" ("The Young Yeats," in *The Shaping of Modern Ireland*, ed. Conor Cruise O'Brien [Toronto: Toronto University Press, 1960], p. 148).

7. "A. E.," review of *A Memoir of A. E. (George William Russell)* by John Eglinton, and *The Living Torch, by A. E.*, ed. Monk Gibbon, *The New Statesman and Nation*, 4 Dec. 1937, p. 958.

8. *A Portrait of the Artist as a Young Man* (1916; rpt. New York: The Viking Press, 1956), p. 203.

9. A comment made by the poet John Montague in 1957 is

revealing. In a "Letter from Dublin," published in the important American journal *Poetry* (95, No. 5 [1957]: 311), Montague called Kavanagh "unquestionably our finest poet," and labeled Clarke "the acknowledged leader of the 'neo-Gaelic' group."

10. Quoted in *Irish Literary Portraits*, ed. W. R. Rodgers (London: British Broadcasting Corp., 1972), p. 19.

11. The Irish poet Monk Gibbon, who knew both Yeats and Clarke well, says that Yeats's quarrels with Clarke and other writers in A. E.'s circle were "subtly linked with the devotion which these men showed to his [Yeats's] boyhood companion" (*The Masterpiece and the Man: Yeats as I Knew Him* [London: Rupert Hart-Davis, 1959], p. 52). Gibbon also said, in a personal interview, that the sudden acclaim won by *The Vengeance of Fionn* fed Yeats's jealousy of writers who might challenge his status as Ireland's leading poet.

According to Frank O'Connor, Yeats read Clarke's first novel, *The Bright Temptation* (1932), "with genuine admiration" (quoted in *Irish Literary Portraits*, p. 192), and Yeats, in a letter to Olivia Shakespear, recommended the book as "a charming and humorous defiance of the censorship and its ideals" (*The Letters of W. B. Yeats*, ed. Allan Wade [London: Rupert Hart-Davis, 1954], p. 795). (Yeats's famous arrogance shows through, however, in another comment about Clarke's book in the same letter: "Read it and tell me should I make him an Academician [a member of the Irish Academy of Letters]. I find it very difficult to see, with impartial eyes, these Irish writers who are as it were part of my propaganda.") Yeats rejected Clarke's first play (later published as *The Son of Learning*) when it was submitted to the Abbey.

12. *Letters to the New Island*, ed. Horace Reynolds (Cambridge, Mass.: Harvard University Press, 1934), p. 174; quoted in Phillip L. Marcus, *Yeats and the Beginning of the Irish Renaissance* (Ithaca, N.Y.: Cornell University Press, 1970), p. 16.

13. "The Parish and the Universe," in Patrick Kavanagh, *Collected Pruse* [*sic*] (London: Macgibbon & Kee, 1967), pp. 282–283.

14. The phrase "humanistic vision" is, I realize, a slippery one. In my use of it and of the term "humanism" throughout this work, I am not referring specifically to the Christian humanism of the Renaissance nor to the atheistic humanism of the twentieth century, but rather to a general point of view that takes man as the center of the universe and the measure of all things, and that looks to this world

rather than to worlds to come as the most important arena of man's endeavors.

15. *Salve*, Vol. II of *Hail and Farewell!* (London: William Heinemann, 1912), p. 118. Augustine Martin, in "The Rediscovery of Austin Clarke" (p. 420), describes Clarke's religious upbringing this way: "It is fair to say that what the young Austin Clarke received and rejected was not a Catholic education, but an unusually pestilent mixture of Victorian and Jansenist prejudice, reinforced by contemporary, pseudo-medical superstition about the dangers—especially to sanity—of self-abuse. It is also fair to say that such an education was, apparently, not untypical of its time and place."

16. *Twice Round the Black Church: Early Memories of Ireland and England* (London: Routledge & Kegan Paul, 1962), p. 132.

17. Ibid., p. 10.

18. Ibid.

19. Ibid., pp. 26–27. The Sixth Commandment states, "Thou shalt not commit adultery."

20. *A Portrait of the Artist as a Young Man*, p. 142.

21. M. D. [Maurice Devane, pseudonym for Austin Clarke], review of *Horizon: A Review of Literature and Art*, ed. Cyril Connolly, *The Dublin Magazine*, NS 17, No. 2 (April–June 1942): 66. Actually, Clarke's response to modernism was far more complex than this comment might suggest. It was also, given Clarke's overriding commitment to the Irish tradition, far more informed than might be expected.

In 1920, Clarke married a writer named Geraldine Cummins; the marriage took place not in a Catholic church, but in the Dublin registry office. Such a conspicuous denial of the Church's authority apparently cost Clarke his teaching job at University College, Dublin, where he had been given the post formerly held by his friend and mentor, Thomas MacDonagh, shot for his part in the Easter Rising. (It must be added that the "evidence" that Clarke's dismissal was a direct result of his marriage comes only from Clarke himself, in *Twice Round the Black Church*, p. 90.) And so Clarke went, as so many other Irishmen before him had done, to London; he arrived in 1922, just in time to take advantage of the last few prosperous years of the great Fleet Street tradition of book reviewing, and just in time (it was the year that *The Waste Land* and *Ulysses* were published) to witness firsthand the modernist revolution in English literature. For fifteen years, Clarke lived in or near London, and made his living chiefly by reviewing books for a variety of influential British publications—among them, *The New Statesman*, *The Nation*, *The London Mercury*, and *The Spectator*. In these years, and in the years after he returned to Ireland in 1937, Clarke had occasion to review everything from Joyce's *Finnegans Wake* to Pound's *Cantos* and Eliot's plays.

On the whole, Clarke found modernist writing confused and uncertain, both in style and in subject matter. In his view, the center of modern British poetry lay much closer to the relatively traditional work of Hardy, Kipling, Graves, and the Georgians than to the radically untraditional work of Eliot and Pound—an argument which, in view of the development of British poetry after Eliot, was more than a little prophetic. Clarke did admire the work of some modernists in drama, particularly the verse plays of Eliot, Auden, and MacLeish. Moreover, one could argue that Clarke's own poetry owes much to the poets of the 1920s and 1930s whom he often objected to in his critical reviews. The highly compressed syntax and sudden shifts in imagery in much of Clarke's later poetry, for example, would seem to be indebted somewhat to poems like *The Waste Land*; Clarke's interest in wit and in poetry with a sharp intellectual edge may owe more than a little to the modernists' revival of interest in seventeenth-century poets like John Donne; and Clarke's stance in the 1950s and 1960s as a public poet committed to commenting on his social and political world would seem to bear the imprint of some of the English poets writing in the 1930s whose sincerity he had called into question.

But in the end, an important truth lies beneath Clarke's rejection of the myriad movements and countermovements that he wrote about as a professional reviewer in the 1920s and 1930s. Clarke could fully embrace neither Anglo-American modernism, of whatever variety, nor the early, more conscientiously Irish work of Yeats, because both seemed, at bottom, either irrelevant or false to the one thing that Clarke held dear: The Irish experience as he saw it—that is, the Catholic and Gaelic experience.

22. *A Penny in the Clouds*, p. 51.

2. "A Mad Discordancy": Early Narrative Poems

1. See Appendix for texts of these poems, which were published in 1916 and early 1917 in *New Ireland* but which have not been collected.

2. Quoted in Susan Halpern, *Austin Clarke, His Life and Works* (Dublin: Dolmen Press, 1974), p. 42.

3. "Some Recent Irish Books," review of *The Vengeance of Fionn* and others, *Studies* 7, No. 25 (1918): 179–180.

4. "The Vengeance of Fionn," *The Times Literary Supplement*, 18 Jan. 1918, p. 30.

5. "The New Epic," review of *The Vengeance of Fionn*, *New Ireland*, 2 March 1918, p. 273.

6. "I, Said the Quarterly," *New Ireland*, 9 March 1918, p. 292.

7. The poet James Stephens contributed to the dispute with a Letter to the Editor, *New Ireland*, 16 March 1918, pp. 307–308. Campbell also wrote a letter that was published under the heading, "An Open Letter to Stephen MacKenna," in *New Ireland*, 16 March 1918, p. 307, to which MacKenna replied in a letter published in *New Ireland*, 30 March 1918, pp. 340–341. Two other participants in the dispute were Boirin Ni Shionnaigh, whose letter was published in *New Ireland*, 23 March 1918, p. 326, and Herbert Moore Pim, whose letter was published in *New Ireland*, 30 March 1918, p. 341.

8. *A Penny in the Clouds: More Memories of Ireland and England* (London: Routledge & Kegan Paul, 1968), p. 90.

9. An example is George Brandon Saul's essay, "The Poetry of Austin Clarke," in *The Celtic Cross: Studies in Irish Culture and Literature*, eds. Ray B. Browne et al. (Lafayette, Ind.: Purdue University Studies, 1964). Saul calls *The Vengeance of Fionn* "occasionally inspired prentice work" (p. 27) and attacks it as verbose, awkward in meter, poorly structured, and overly descriptive (pp. 27–28).

10. Thomas Kinsella excluded *The Vengeance of Fionn*, and Clarke's three other early narrative poems, from his *Austin Clarke: Selected Poems* (Dublin: Dolmen Press, 1976), calling them products of "Clarke's apprenticeship" (p. xii).

11. Ferguson wrote about the death of Diarmuid in *Lays of the Western Gael* (1865). Katherine Tynan published "The Pursuit of Diarmuid and Grainne," a long narrative poem written in various stanzaic and metric patterns, in 1887. The text of Yeats's and Moore's play, *Diarmuid and Grania*, was not published until 1951, when it appeared in *The Dublin Magazine* 26, No. 2 (April–June 1951). Lady Gregory included a translation of the original Gaelic tale, *Toraigheact Dhiarmada agus Ghrainne*, in her *Gods and Fighting Men* (1904). Her play *Grania* was written in 1911 and published in 1912.

12. All quotations of Clarke's poetry are from *Austin Clarke: Collected Poems*, ed. Liam Miller (Dublin: Dolmen Press; London and New York: Oxford Univ. Press, 1974), hereafter cited as *CP*.

13. *A Penny in the Clouds*, p. 167.

14. The style of *Deirdre Wed* parallels that of *The Vengeance of Fionn* as much as does the story that it tells. It suffers from the same cluttered imagery and dense description, but also exhibits some of the more admirable qualities of Clarke's poem, as evidenced in this passage, describing the house of Connachar, high king, on the night of Deirdre's wedding:

> . . . For now
> Hundreds with ruddy-glistening faces ran
> Jostling round the nine shadows of the blaze
> And spread with skins the lengthy beds of men
> And soused warm spice of herbs in ale. Here—thither—
> Was rousing of age-slumber'd horns, arranging
> Smooth banks throughout the house, strawing of rushes,
> And cauldrons humm'd before the empty throne
> Set high in the shadow of the wall, and bubbled
> Inaudible, impatient for the king.
>
> *Poems by Herbert Trench* (London:
> Constable, 1919), I, p. 8

Brendan Kennelly, in "Austin Clarke and the Epic Poem," *Irish University Review* 4, No. 1 (Spring 1974): 29, has shown that Clarke's debt to Trench extends to his dramatic treatment of the narrative.

The objective nature of the Gaelic tradition has been described aptly by Daniel Corkery, the Irish writer and scholar: "This case of hardness is scarcely ever lacking to the Gaelic poet; track him right down the centuries, and one never finds it missing. It is intellectual in its nature: hard-headed and clear-sighted . . . one can turn over the pages of the Gaelic book of poetry, century after century, without coming on any set of verses that one could speak of as sentimental" (*The Hidden Ireland: A Study of Gaelic Munster in the Eighteenth Century* [Dublin: M. H. Gill, 1924, 1967], p. 211).

15. "The Poetry of Herbert Trench," *The London Mercury* 10, No. 56 (1924): 159. "The Ossian of Macpherson" refers to James Macpherson's eighteenth-century "translations" from a poet whom he called "Ossian." The translations became immensely popular,

particularly during the Romantic movement in Europe, and were said to be among Napoleon's favorite poems. It was later discovered, however, that Macpherson, a Scots poet, had not been working from original Gaelic manuscripts, and that his version of the Ossian poems differed markedly from original Gaelic poems about Ossian, a legendary Irish poet. The poems and stories of Fiona Macleod (a pseudonym for the nineteenth-century Scots writer William Sharp) were widely regarded as quintessential Celtic Twilight literature.

The difference between Clarke's commitment to the Gaelic dimension of the Irish tradition and the commitment of Yeats and other leading figures of the literary revival can be seen to some extent by comparing two reactions—one from Clarke and one from George Moore—to Douglas Hyde, the Gaelic scholar whose work influenced both Clarke and the revival. Clarke's reaction appears in *Twice Round the Black Church: Early Memories of Ireland and England* (London: Routledge & Kegan Paul, 1962), p. 169, and describes Clarke's experience as a student of Hyde's at University College, Dublin, where Hyde held a chair in modern Irish:

> As an undergraduate I escaped at one step from the snobbery of school life and discovered the Love Songs of Connaught, those poems and translations which had started our Literary Revival. Their poet-translator was on the rostrum, and, though I could not always follow the swift rush of Dr. Hyde's western Irish I knew from his gestures that he was speaking a living language. When the future President of Eire enacted *Casadh an tSugain* [a play in Irish that Hyde had written], he took the parts of all the characters, jumping up and down from the rostrum in his excitement, and, as he unwound an imaginary straw rope at the end of the play, found himself outside the lecture room.
>
> On the morning of our first term, he spoke of the aims and ideals of the language revival; we were all equal, all united in the Gaelic movement. There was no vulgar competition, no showing-off, no twopence-halfpenny looking down on twopence. Those plain words changed me in a few seconds. The hands of our lost despised centuries were laid on me.

Moore's reaction appears in *Ave*, the first volume of *Hail and Farewell!* (London: William Heinemann, 1911), p. 118, and recalls a dinner party at which Hyde was speaking in English, but then suddenly broke into Irish:

And then a torrent of dark muddied stuff flowed from him, much like the porter which used to come up from Carnacun to be drunk by the peasants on mid-summer nights when a bonfire was lighted. It seemed to me a language suitable for the celebration of an antique Celtic rite, but too remote for modern use. It had never been spoken by ladies in silken gowns with fans in their hands or by gentlemen going out to kill each other with engraved rapiers or pistols. Men had merely cudgelled each other, yelling strange oaths the while in Irish, and I remembered it in the mouths of the old fellows dressed in breeches and worsted stockings, swallowtail coats and tall hats full of dirty bank-notes which they used to give to my father.

Moore's statement certainly makes clear the class distinctions attached to the language. It also makes clear that the literary revival, for all its insistence on returning to the soil of the peasant, was undertaken by men whose aesthetic views and ambitions often put them squarely on the side of the gentlemen with engraved rapiers or pistols. Men like Yeats and Moore were always conscious of the world outside Ireland, a world that could not be reached in the language that Douglas Hyde was arguing for—and conscious of it in a way that a literary separatist like Austin Clarke was not.

16. *The Variorum Edition of the Poems of W. B. Yeats*, eds. Peter Allt and Russell K. Alspach (New York: Macmillan, 1957), pp. 2–3.

17. Augustine Martin, "The Rediscovery of Austin Clarke," *Studies* 54, No. 216 (1965): 410–411, has made this point about *The Vengeance of Fionn* and *The Wanderings of Oisin*. Clarke's first poem, Martin says, "has a firmer sense of reality, a sharper and more definite use of language, a more compelling power to create a world than the soft, dreamy, Italianate texture of Yeats's saga." It must be admitted that, writing in 1917, Clarke may well have profited from the movement, conducted under the banner of modernism and contributed to by Yeats himself, toward a "harder" poetry and away from the kind of aesthetic views that influenced Yeats's early works. Nonetheless, it seems plausible that the qualities of *The Vengeance of Fionn* admired by Martin owe far more to the Gaelic tradition than to what was going on in London at the time.

18. The most recent prose translation of the *Tain*, done by Thomas Kinsella and praised for its accuracy, begins:

Once when the royal bed was laid out for Ailill and Medb in Cruachan fort in Connacht, they had this talk on the pillows:

"It is true what they say, love," Ailill said, "it is well for the wife of a wealthy man."

"True enough," the woman said. "What put that into your mind?"

"It struck me," Ailill said, "how much better off you are today than the day I married you."

"I was well enough off without you," Medb said.

> *The Tain: Translated From the Irish Epic Tain Bo Cuailnge*
> (London: Oxford University Press, 1970), p. 52.

3. "A Court of Judgment on the Soul" (I): *Pilgrimage*

1. *Twice Round the Black Church: Early Memories of Ireland and England* (London: Routledge & Kegan Paul, 1962), p. 19.

2. Augustine Martin is one of the few critics to argue for the poems of *Pilgrimage* and *Night and Morning* over Clarke's later work. In "The Rediscovery of Austin Clarke," *Studies* 54, No. 216 (1965): 416, he says: "These two volumes contain his most intense and moving poems. In them is portrayed the search of an individual soul for clarity and peace; they reveal Mr. Clarke as wrenched between the opposing demands of the flesh and spirit, of religious prohibition and intellectual freedom, between the dark legacy of the Fall and the alternate gaiety of paganism towards which the artist and the humanist in him incline." One other critic, Douglas Sealy, has pointed to Clarke's work in this period, particularly *Night and Morning*, to make the claim for Clarke over Yeats. In "Austin Clarke: A Survey of His Work," *The Dubliner*, No. 6 (Jan.–Feb. 1963): 17, Sealy says: "By concentration on two subjects, freedom of thought and freedom of instinct, he produced the richest verse of any Irishman of our age, not excepting Yeats. The Church is on one side, freedom on the other. And both are in Clarke's mind. The poetry is in the struggle. They are the poems of a soul in torment. Beside this agonizing, Yeats's occultism, astrology, pernes and gyres and phases of the moon, despite the magnificent rhetoric of his poetry, seem shallow indeed."

3. "The Black Church," *The Dublin Magazine*, NS 14, No. 4 (Oct.–Dec. 1939): 13.

4. "Irish Poetry To-Day," *The Dublin Magazine*, NS 10, No. 1

(Jan.–Mar. 1935): 32. The argument that poets should substitute assonance for rhyme was made on metrical grounds in 1894 by the Irish poet William Larminie, whose essay, "The Development of English Metres," *The Contemporary Review* 66 (1894): 717–736, A. E. called to Clarke's attention.

Assonance became important in the Gaelic tradition of poetry only after the Gaelic aristocracy began, in the seventeenth century, to collapse. The decline in the aristocracy led to the disappearance of the *filés*, the highest grade of Gaelic poets, and to a corresponding rise in the importance of the less sophisticated rank of poets known as bards. These bards rejected the complex syllabic meters and consonantal rhyme patterns of the *filés* in favor of accentual meter and vowel-rhyme, or assonance. The result was a great flowering of lyrical verse. Douglas Hyde traces the Gaelic roots of assonance in *A Literary History of Ireland* (London: T. Fisher Unwin, 1899), pp. 539–551. As an example of assonance in bardic verse, Hyde gives his own translation of a poem by an eighteenth-century bard, Tadhg Gaolach O'Sullivan:

> The pOets with lAys are uprAising their nOtes
> In amAze, and they knOw how their tOnes will delight,
> For the gOlden-hair lAdy so grAceful, so pOseful,
> So gAElic, so glOrious enthrOned in our sight.
> UnfOlding a tAle, how the sOul of a fAy must
> Be clOthed in the frAme of a lAdy so bright,
> UntOld are her grAces, a rOse in her fAce is
> And nO man so stAid is but fAints at her sight.
>
> p. 548, emphasis Hyde's

The variation of "o" and "a" sounds within each line recalls the patterns of internal assonance in Clarke's "The Straying Student." Clarke's practice of echoing a word at the end of one line with a word in the middle of the following line ("On pale knees in the *dawn*, / Parting the *straw* that wrapped me") can be traced to a popular Gaelic meter called Great Rannaigheact, also illustrated by Hyde in a translation, using rhyme rather than assonance:

> To hear handsome women *weep*,
> In *deep* distress sobbing sore.
>
> (p. 531)

5. "The Black Church," p. 11.

6. Note to "The Young Woman of Beare," *Later Poems* (Dublin: Dolmen Press, 1961), p. 90.

7. The association of this image with pagan fertility ritual is made by Frederick A. Kalister, "Eternal Absolution: The Poetry of Austin Clarke" (Diss., Ohio University, 1971), p. 34.

8. Clarke might well have found Gormlai's story in George Sigerson, *Bards of the Gael and Gall* (1897; rpt. New York: Charles Scribner's Sons, 1907). Sigerson, a man whom Clarke admired, included in his book a translation of "Niall's Dirge," a poem spoken by Gormlai (p. 194), and a brief account of her life in an appendix (pp. 413–415). Clarke also used the story of Gormlai in his second prose romance, *The Singing-Men at Cashel* (London: George Allen & Unwin, 1936).

9. This point is made explicitly in *The Singing-Men at Cashel*. After visiting the monk Benignus, seeking counsel and being told only that she should do her duty by Carrol, Gormlai rebels: "Her mind answered in revolt, denying the wisdom of his age and experience. That night when Nial and she stood outside the wood, she had known that all was different, that they were on the verge of some imaginative reality in which her heart still believed, that they had not been driven together by a common sensuality. No, no, it was not an ignoble impulse, a cunning deception of sin. Her entire mind rushed into that moment, and was changed, finding that ancient truth for which it sought" (p. 298).

10. This point has been argued by Maurice Harmon, "The Later Poetry of Austin Clarke," in *The Celtic Cross: Studies in Irish Culture and Literature*, eds. Ray B. Browne et al. (Lafayette, Ind.: Purdue University Studies, 1964), pp. 413–414.

11. A translation of "The Old Woman of Beare" by Kuno Meyer, the German scholar whose research contributed importantly to the Irish literary revival, appears in *1000 Years of Irish Poetry: The Gaelic and Anglo-Irish Poets from Pagan Times to the Present*, ed. Kathleen Hoagland (New York: Devan-Adair, 1947), pp. 39–42.

12. The original Irish poem has been reprinted in *Measgra Dánta: Miscellaneous Irish Poems*, ed. Thomas F. O'Rahilly (Dublin and Cork: Cork University Press, 1927), pp. 16–17.

13. The poems are "South-Westerly Gale," "The Marriage Night," "The Planter's Daughter," and "Aisling."

14. In *Austin Clarke: Collected Poems*, ed. Liam Miller (Dublin: Dolmen Press; London and New York: Oxford University Press, 1974), "Wandering Men" is inexplicably grouped with several lyrics first published in Clarke's *Collected Poems* of 1936.

15. The note, which appeared in *The Collected Poems of Austin Clarke* (New York: Macmillan, 1936), p. 312, says: "Many of the miracles attributed to St. Brigid are of a curious visional quality and deal with mental phenomena. This is interesting in view of the fact that there has been some confusion in legend between the saint and the early Brigid, the goddess of Fire and Poetic Inspiration."

16. Robert Farren, *The Course of Irish Verse in English* (New York: Sheed & Ward, 1947), p. 156, has pointed out the assonantal patterns in this stanza.

4. "A Court of Judgment on the Soul" (II): *Night and Morning*

1. "A Note on Austin Clarke," *The Dublin Magazine*, NS 5, No. 2 (April–June 1930): 67.

2. *Twice Round the Black Church: Early Memories of Ireland and England* (London: Routledge & Kegan Paul, 1962), p. 14.

3. Ibid., p. 174.

4. Douglas Sealy, "Austin Clarke: A Survey of His Work," *The Dubliner*, No. 6 (Jan.–Feb. 1963): 18, has pointed out this reference.

5. *The London Mercury* 35, No. 210 (1937): 550–551.

6. Daniel J. Murphy, "The Religious Lyrics and Satires of Austin Clarke," *Hermathena* 122 (1977): 54, makes an interesting observation on these lines: "Many of Clarke's poems bear witness also to the survival in his thought not only of some of the formal elements of Catholicism, such as its liturgical symbols and the semi-mystical dimensions of its ritual, but, to some degree, of its intellectual methods as well. The 'borrowed robe' of the mind is the metaphor used to suggest this in 'Night and Morning.' His thought is, to some extent, shaped by forces which his reason urges him to reject." This is perhaps most evident in the penultimate stanza of "Ancient Lights," discussed at the end of this chapter.

7. Vivian Mercier, "Mortal Anguish, Mortal Pride: Austin Clarke's Religious Lyrics," *Irish University Review* 4, No. 1 (Spring 1974): 94, has pointed out this pun.

8. "Austin Clarke and Padraic Fallon," in *Two Decades of Irish*

Writing: A Critical Survey, ed. Douglas Dunn (Cheadle: Carcanet Press, 1975), p. 45.

9. Ibid., p. 46.

10. I owe this second reading of these lines to a conversation with Donald Davie.

11. "The Rediscovery of Austin Clarke," *Studies* 54, No. 216 (1965): 418.

12. Martin, ibid., pp. 417–418, has said of this stanza: "A reader coming unexpectedly on this stanza is, I suggest, surprised by an unusual sense of melody and counterpoint which cannot be accounted for by rhyme or the more conventional euphonies of English verse."

13. "The Writers: Austin Clarke," R. T. E. Television, 29 Jan. 1968.

14. "The Rediscovery of Austin Clarke," p. 419. Martin comments on how the language in this stanza contributes to the effect, noting "the calculated vagueness of 'they say' and 'a college wall in France' " and "how the whole world of ecclesiastical discipline is subtly elided from his [the student's] consciousness, and the usurping influence of artistic wonder is faded in."

15. Martin, ibid., takes this view to some extent, arguing that "Ancient Lights" represents a "catharsis for which he [Clarke] has looked in vain" (p. 421) and which "projects Clarke into a new phase of creativity" (p. 424). Thomas Kinsella goes dangerously further. "In 1955, with *Ancient Lights*, he [Clarke] emerges from silence in sudden, full-fledged humanitarian rage," Kinsella says in "The Poetic Career of Austin Clarke," *Irish University Review* 4, No. 1 (Spring 1974): 134. "The struggles of conscience are over—sluiced away in "Ancient Lights"—and a fund of energy is released, outward and inward."

16. *Twice Round the Black Church*, pp. 138–139.

17. In his review of *Ancient Lights* (*Irish Writing*, No. 34 [Spring 1956]: 57–58), Donald Davie singled out this stanza as an example of Clarke's stylistic powers. "There are few poets now writing in English," Davie said, "who are capable of such a stanza, so continuously inventive in detail yet so sure of total effect, so strenuous and surprising in diction yet running so free, so much at ease yet so tightly organized." Noting the attention that Davie paid to this stanza,

Augustine Martin, "The Rediscovery of Austin Clarke," p. 423, attempted a more detailed explanation:

> Again it is worth pausing to examine the detail that has contributed to produce such a rich finality of utterance. The prosody is Austin Clarke at his simplest: unrhymed iambic dimeter reinforced by a flexible accent: hence "up" is answered by "gutters," "mocked" by "ballcocks," "sparrowing" seeks an extra and strenuous echo in "swallowing." The freedom of movement which this simple pattern permits could not be achieved with conventional rhyme and end-stop. But the metrics are insignificant beside the remarkable use of language and symbol. The simple descriptive impact of the poem, the freshness with which it describes the sun coming out after a cloudburst is so arresting that one might overlook the inner, psychological process which it triggers and parallels.

(Martin apparently is using the term "dimeter" in a way that differs from standard prosodic terminology; the stanza is written in tetrameter lines.)

18. James Joyce, *A Portrait of the Artist as a Young Man* (1916; rpt. New York: The Viking Press, 1956), p. 240.

5. "The World's Mad Business" (I): Shorter Public Poems

1. *Twice Round the Black Church: Early Memories of Ireland and England* (London: Routledge & Kegan Paul, 1962), p. 95.

2. The poem was published in *The Dublin Magazine*, NS 16, No. 1 (Jan.–March 1941): 1, in the following form:

"Celebrations"
Who dare complain or be ashamed
Of liberties our arms have taken?
For every spike upon that gateway,
We have uncrowned the past
And open hearts are celebrating
Prosperity of church and state
In the shade of Dublin Castle.

So many flagpoles can be seen now
Blessing the crowd, baring the forehead

While the dancing keys at College Green
Treble the wards of nation,
God only knows what treasury
Pours down to keep each city borough
And thoroughfare in grace.

Our ageing politicians pray
Again, the hoardings blacken with faith,
The blindfold woman in a rage
Condemns her own for treason:
No steeple topped the scale that day
Youthful souls had lost their savings
And looters ran the street.

This poem has received considerable critical attention, and my discussion of it is particularly indebted to the insights of Seamus Cooney's "Austin Clarke's 'Celebrations': A Commentary," *Eire-Ireland* 2, No. 2 (Summer 1967): 16–26, and of Maurice Harmon's "The Later Poetry of Austin Clarke," in *The Celtic Cross: Studies in Irish Culture and Literature*, eds. Ray B. Browne et al. (Lafayette, Ind.: Purdue University Studies, 1964), pp. 49–52.

3. Part of Clarke's note to the poem also suggests this reading: "Over the gateway of Dublin Castle there is a statue of Justice. During the Civil War, seventy Republicans were executed by the Provisional Government. Between 1936–46, when the Republican Government was in power, of the small group of political intransigents, four were shot without trial, four were shot by firing squad, one was hanged by Pierpoint, and three died on hunger strike" (*CP*, 548).

4. *Twice Round the Black Church*, p. 121.

5. Augustine Martin, in "The Rediscovery of Austin Clarke," *Studies* 54, No. 216 (1965): 433, has made the point that this poem is about discrimination in general.

6. Clark began experimenting with many of these poetic devices, particularly various patterns and kinds of rhyme, in the plays that he wrote between his return to Ireland in 1937 and the publication of *Ancient Lights* in 1955. In *The Kiss* (1942), he uses assonance along with internal and terminal rhyme; in *The Viscount of Blarney* (1944), he uses rhyme, particularly between words in medial positions in successive lines; in *The Second Kiss* (1946), he uses double and triple rhymes for humorous effect; and in *The Plot Succeeds* (1950), he uses heroic couplets.

7. The most detailed treatment of the poem is Horst Oppel, "Austin Clarke: 'Three Poems About Children (III),' " in *Die Moderne Englische Lyrik: Interpretationem*, ed. Horst Oppel (Berlin: Erich Schmidt Verlag, 1967), pp. 262–268. Donald Davie, "Austin Clarke and Padraic Fallon," in *Two Decades of Irish Writing: A Critical Survey*, ed. Douglas Dunn (Cheadle: Carcanet Press, 1975), p. 48, cites the third poem in the sequence as an example of "the direct savagery of the lampoon." Charles Tomlinson discusses the poem as an example of narrowly focused nationalistic poetry in "Poetry Today," in *The Modern Age: Volume 7 of the Pelican Guide to English Literature*, ed. Boris Ford (Harmondsworth: Penguin Books, 1961, 1964), pp. 460–461. Maurice Harmon, "The Later Poetry of Austin Clarke," pp. 52–53, discusses the third poem in relation to the other two, but briefly.

8. Oppel, "Austin Clarke," p. 264, makes this point, and Harmon, "The Later Poetry of Austin Clarke," pp. 52–53, suggests it.

6. "The World's Mad Business" (II): Longer Public Poems

1. Poems that belong to this category are "The Loss of Strength" (*Too Great a Vine*), "The Flock at Dawn" (*The Horse-Eaters*), "The Hippophagi" (*The Horse-Eaters*), "Forget Me Not" (1962), "Cypress Grove" (*Flight to Africa*), and "Beyond the Pale" (*Flight to Africa*).

2. In a note to the poem, Clarke says: "*Loss of Strength* was suggested by a dangerous illness and by Coleridge's poem, *Youth and Age*.

> This body that does me grievous wrong
> O'er aery cliffs and glittering sands
> How lightly *then* it flashed along."
>   (*CP*, 550)

Two years after "The Loss of Strength" was published, Clarke suffered a severe heart attack. (Maurice Harmon, "Notes Toward a Biography," *Irish University Review* 4, No. 1 [Spring 1974]: 24.)

3. William John Roscelli, "The Private Pilgrimage of Austin Clarke," in *The Celtic Cross: Studies in Irish Culture and Literature*, eds. Ray B. Browne et al. (Lafayette, Ind.: Purdue University Studies, 1964), p. 69, says in a footnote to his discussion of "Forget Me Not": "I have seen too many people dying of starvation in Shimbashi slums to become greatly exercised over man's inhumanity to horses. If

an export horse trade can boost a nation's economy and help eliminate poverty, I find nothing short-sighted or stupid in it, Lemuel Gulliver and Austin Clarke notwithstanding." Donald Davie, "Austin Clarke and Padraic Fallon," in *Two Decades of Irish Writing: A Critical Survey*, ed. Douglas Dunn (Cheadle: Carcanet Press, 1975), p. 49, replies quite rightly that this "bluff humanitarian good sense is beside the point."

4. "Austin Clarke and Padraic Fallon," p. 50.

5. Ibid.

6. Ibid.

7. In *Twice Round the Black Church: Early Memories of Ireland and England* (London: Routledge & Kegan Paul, 1962), pp. 53–54, Clarke recalls boyhood afternoons spent watching the horse traffic outside his house on Mountjoy Street:

> The main event every day in our street occurred at half past five in the evening, when, in rapid succession, cabs and outside cars came up St. Mary's Place, around the far side of the Black Church, on the way to meet the Galway train. They raced past the open gates of the private road, opposite the Church, which led to Broadstone Station. Not long afterwards, they swept back again, with clatter, jingle and tattle of harness, past our side of St. Mary's Place. Although most of them had travellers, a cab or outside car, sometimes, came back empty, but always the horse held its head up bravely.

8. Vivian Mercier, *The Irish Comic Tradition* (Oxford: Clarendon Press, 1962), pp. 191–193, argues that Swift, although he was Anglo-Irish and could not read Gaelic, exhibits in his satirical work many qualities of the ancient tradition of satire in the Irish language. Since Clarke knew both the language and its literature, one might wonder how much his satirical work owes to this tradition. He certainly was aware of it; for example, *Aislinge Meic Conglinne*, the twelfth-century Irish poem that Clarke used as a basis for his first play, *The Son of Learning*, is an important exhibit in the Irish satirical tradition. Moreover, some of the characteristics of satire in Irish—its extravagant anger, its use of the grotesque, and, above all, what Mercier calls its "verbal virtuosity" (p. 7)—can be found in Clarke's satirical verse.

9. The Swift poem that Clarke is referring to is "The Day of Judgment," published in 1731, near the end of Swift's life:

With a whirl of thought oppress'd,
I sunk from reverie to rest.
A horrid vision seized my head,
I saw the graves give up their dead!
Jove, arm'd with terrors, bursts the skies,
And thunder roars and lightning flies!
Amazed, confused, its fate unknown,
The world stands trembling at his throne!
While each pale sinner hung his head,
Jove, nodding, shook the heavens, and said:
"Offending race of human kind,
By nature, reason, learning, blind;
You who, through frailty, stepp'd aside;
And you, who never fell from pride:
You who in different sects were shamm'd,
And come to see each other damn'd;
(So some folk told you, but they knew
No more of Jove's designs than you;)
—The world's mad business now is o'er,
And I resent these pranks no more.
—I to such blockheads set my wit!
I damn such fools!—Go, go, you're bit."

From *The Poems of Jonathan Swift: Selected*,
introd. Padraic Colum (New York: Collier
Books, 1962), p. 125

7. "The Oracle, Not Yet Dumb" (I): *Mnemosyne Lay in Dust*

1. *Later Poems* (Dublin: Dolmen Press, 1961) reprinted the poems from *Pilgrimage* (1929), *Night and Morning* (1938), *Ancient Lights* (1955), *Too Great a Vine* (1957), and *The Horse-Eaters* (1960).

2. "One More Brevity," in *A Tribute to Austin Clarke on His Seventieth Birthday: 9 May 1966*, eds. John Montague and Liam Miller (Dublin: Dolmen Press, 1966), p. 21.

3. Other later poems that belong, at least in part, to this category include "From a Diary of Dreams," "The Knock," "The Jest," "Every Fine Day," "Following Darkness," and "The Plot" from *Flight To Africa*; "Old-Fashioned Pilgrimage" and "More Extracts From a Diary of Dreams" from *Old-Fashioned Pilgrimage*; and "The Echo at

Coole," "F. R. Higgins," and "Impotence" from *The Echo at Coole*.

4. *Twice Round the Black Church: Early Memories of Ireland and England* (London: Routledge & Kegan Paul, 1962), pp. 7–8.

5. *A Penny in the Clouds: More Memories of Ireland and England* (London: Routledge & Kegan Paul, 1968), p. 43.

6. Robert F. Garratt, "The Poetry of Austin Clarke" (Diss., University of Oregon, 1972), pp. 133–134, has noted that the loss of pronouns in "heart" and "body" helps create "a sense of impersonality" in this stanza.

7. *Twice Round the Black Church*, pp. 89–90.

8. Literally, the verb "stell" means to fix one's eyes or to have a fixed stare. The sense of the word as used here is that the sound of the stream mesmerized Maurice. The word comes from the Old English word "stellan," or "stiellan," meaning to establish or fix.

9. Basil Payne, "Vigour and Technical Virtuosity," review of *Mnemosyne Lay in Dust* by Austin Clarke and *A Tribute to Austin Clarke on his Seventieth Birthday*, eds. John Montague and Liam Miller, *Hibernia* 30, No. 6 (June 1966): 12.

10. M. L. Rosenthal, review of *Austin Clarke: Selected Poems*, ed. Thomas Kinsella, *A Slow Dance* by John Montague, and *The New Estate* by Ciaran Carson, *The New York Times Book Review*, 19 September 1976, p. 6.

11. Maurice Harmon, review of *Mnemosyne Lay in Dust* by Austin Clarke and *A Tribute to Austin Clarke on His Seventieth Birthday*, eds. John Montague and Liam Miller, *Studies* 55, No. 219 (1966): 327, makes this argument: "He [Maurice Devane] is close to the typical twentieth-century figure, the anti-hero shorn of traditional supports. By plunging him into the isolation of the mental hospital, Clarke reduces him to the condition of a Beckett hero, denies him a place in the sun and brings him face to face with the void, with nothingness."

8. "The Oracle, Not Yet Dumb" (II): Late Erotic Poems

1. The story of the Dagda is told in the Irish tale "Cath Maige Tured" ("The [Second] Battle of Moytura"). A translation by Whitley Stokes appears in *Revue Celtique* 12 (1891): 52–130, but it omits the scene of lovemaking that Clarke's poem focuses on. Clarke would have found Stokes's explanation for this omission most interesting: "Here is omitted an account of the meeting of the Dagdae and the

daughter of Indech under difficulties caused by the distention of the Dagdae's stomach. Much of it is obscure to me, and much of the rest is too indecent to be published in this *Revue*" (p. 86).

2. The Irish text of the tale has been edited by Brian ó Cuív, and reprinted in *Celtica* 2 (1954): 325–333.

3. This translation, by David Greene, is quoted in Vivian Mercier, *The Irish Comic Tradition* (Oxford: Clarendon Press, 1962), pp. 41–42.

4. Quoted in Mercier, p. 41.

9. "The Oracle, Not Yet Dumb" (III): Gaelic Translations

1. "The Rediscovery of Austin Clarke," *Studies* 54, No. 216 (1965): 409.

2. The Irish text is printed in *Amhrain Chearbhalláin: The Poems of Carolan*, ed. Tomás O'Máille (London: The Irish Texts Society, 1916), pp. 109–111. A translation by Charlotte Brook appeared in *Reliques of Irish Poetry*, trans. Charlotte Brook (Dublin: George Bonham, 1789), pp. 250–254. A version by Thomas Furlong was published in *Irish Minstrelsy, or Bardic Remains of Ireland*, ed. James Hardiman (1831; rpt. New York: Barnes & Noble, 1971), pp. 62–63. George Sigerson's translation appeared in Sigerson, *Bards of the Gael and Gall*, 2nd ed. (New York: Charles Scribner's Sons, 1907), pp. 256–258.

3. Robert Welch, "Austin Clarke and Gaelic Poetic Tradition," *Irish University Review* 4, No. 1 (Spring 1974): 47–48, has argued this point. Clarke, in *A Penny in the Clouds: More Memories of Ireland and England* (London: Routledge & Kegan Paul, 1968), p. 21, says that Stephen MacKenna first acquainted him with what he calls the "occasional, irregular" rhythms of O'Carolan.

4. See *A Penny in the Clouds*, pp. 42–43.

5. *Bards of the Gael and Gall*, p. 257.

6. Some sense of O'Carolan's irregular rhythms and assonantal sound patterns can be gained by looking at the first stanza of the original, from *Amhráin Chearbhalláin*, p. 109:

Ciabí a mbeith sé (i) ndán dó
  A lámh dheas fháil faoi n-a ceann,
Is deimhin liom nárbh eagal bás dó,
  Choidhche go bráth na ina bheo bheith tinn.

A chúl deas na mbachall fáinneach, fionn,
    A chum mar an 'ala is gile (a') snámh air a' tuinn:
Grádh agus speis gach gasraidh Máible shéimh Ni Cheallaigh,
    Déad is deise leagadh i n-árus a cinn.

In *A Penny in the Clouds*, Clarke says that Sigerson's translations in *Bards of the Gael and Gall* were "already old-fashioned, since the poet in his literary version used double rhyme and jingling internal rhyme" (p. 42.).

7. A literal translation of the passage in O'Carolan, for which I am partly indebted to John Morrissey, is "She has the nicest palm of the hand, foot, arm, and mouth, / And her pair of eyes, and her hair growing halfway to the ground."

8. "Austin Clarke," *The New York Times Book Review*, 7 March 1976, p. 30.

9. The original Irish text, "Pléaráca na Ruarcach," is reprinted along with a prose translation in *Songs of the Irish*, ed. Donal O'Sullivan (New York: Crown Publishers, 1960), pp. 188–189. O'Sullivan also reprints Charles Wilson's translation, "O'Rourke's Feast," first published in his *Select Irish Poems* (1782) and also reprinted in *The Faber Book of Irish Verse*, ed. John Montague (London: Faber & Faber, 1974), pp. 175–176. Jonathan Swift translated the first three stanzas of the poem, entitling it "The Description of an Irish Feast."

10. "The Description of an Irish Feast," *The Poems of Jonathan Swift, Selected*, introd. Padraic Colum (New York: Collier Books, 1962), p. 36.

11. "The Poetry of Swift," in *Jonathan Swift, 1667–1967: A Dublin Tercentenary Tribute*, eds. Roger McHugh and Philip Edwards (Dublin: Dolmen Press, 1967), p. 111.

12. The original poem, "Amhrán na Leabhar" ("Song of the Books"), is printed in *Amhráin Thomáis Ruadh O'Sullivan: The Songs of Tomás Ruadh O'Sullivan*, ed. Seamus Dubh (Dublin: M. H. Gill & Son, 1914), pp. 43–49.

13. The first stanza of the original (from *Amhráin Thomáis Ruadh O'Sullivan*, p. 43) shows how closely Clarke followed O'Sullivan's stanzaic structure and his assonance and rhyme patterns:

Go cuan bhéil ínse casadh me,
Cois Góilin aoibhinn Dairbhre—

Mar a seóltar flít na fairrge
   Thar sáile i gcéin.
I bPortmagee do stadas seal
Fé thuairim intinn maitheasa
D'fhonn bheith sealad eadartha
   Mar mháighistir léighinn;
Is gearr gur chuala an eachtra
   Ag cách, mo léan!
Gur i mBórd Eoghain Fhinn do cailleadh teas,
   An t-árthach tréan.
Do phreab mo chroidhe le hathtuirse
'Dtaoibh loinge an tigheasaigh chalma,
Go mb'fhearrde an tír i sheasamh seal
   Do sáibh an tréin.

14. *The Hidden Ireland: A Study of Gaelic Munster in the Eighteenth Century* (1924; rpt. Dublin: Gill & Macmillan, 1967), p. 184.

15. Clarke wrote three Aislings: one published in *Pilgrimage* (*CP*, 173–175), one published in *Flight to Africa* (*CP*, 299–300), and one published in *The Echo at Coole* (*CP*, 445–446).

Epilogue

1. *A Penny in the Clouds: More Memories of Ireland and England* (London: Routledge & Kegan Paul, 1968), p. 31.

2. This translation is included in MacDonagh's critical study, *Literature in Ireland: Studies Irish and Anglo-Irish* (New York: Frederick A. Stokes, 1916), pp. 146–147.

3. Quoted in George Dangerfield, *The Damnable Question: A Study in Anglo-Irish Relations* (Boston: Little, Brown, 1976), p. 133.

4. *A Penny in the Clouds*, p. 25.

5. *Literature in Ireland*, pp. 32–33.

6. Ibid., pp. 137–138.

A Checklist of Austin Clarke's Poetry

The Vengeance of Fionn. Dublin and London, 1917.

The Fires of Baal. Dublin and London, 1921.

The Cattledrive in Connaught and Other Poems. London, 1925.

Pilgrimage and Other Poems. London, 1929; New York, 1930.

The Collected Poems of Austin Clarke, with an introduction by Padraic Colum. London and New York, 1936. Contains A.C.'s revisions of his early poetry, with two verse plays.

Night and Morning. Dublin, 1938.

The Straying Student. (A poem.) Dublin, 1944.

Ancient Lights, poems and satires: first series. Dublin, 1955.

Too Great a Vine, poems and satires: second series. Dublin, 1957.

The Horse Eaters, poems and satires: third series. Dublin, 1960.

Later Poems. Dublin, 1961. Poems from *Pilgrimage, Night and Morning, Ancient Lights, Too Great a Vine, The Horse Eaters.*

Forget Me Not. Dublin, 1962.

Flight to Africa and Other Poems. Dublin, 1963.

Mnemosyne Lay in Dust. Dublin, 1966.

Old-Fashioned Pilgrimage and Other Poems. Dublin, 1967.

The Echo at Coole and Other Poems. Dublin, 1968.

A Sermon on Swift and Other Poems. Dublin, 1968.

Orphide and Other Poems. Dublin, 1970.

Tiresias. Dublin, 1971.

Collected Poems. Dublin, London and New York, 1974. This included the first printing of "The Wooing of Becfola" and A.C.'s revisions to his earlier narrative poetry. It was subsequently issued in three paperback volumes in October 1974: *Poems 1917–1938; Poems 1955–1966; Poems 1955–1974.*

Selected Poems, edited with an introduction by Thomas Kinsella, Dublin and Winston-Salem, N.C., 1976.

Index

DATE DUE